# A-Level Year 1 & AS

# Biology

## Exam Board: AQA

AS Biology exams can seem pretty daunting unless you get plenty of practice at answering exam-style questions — and, oh, would you look at that — this fabulous CGP Workbook is full of them.

The whole AS Biology course (and Year 1 of A-Level) is covered, with a wide range of questions to really test your wits. Full answers are included, along with top tips to help you grab all the marks you can when the big day comes.

By the time you've worked your way through all this, the real exams should have no impact on your ventricular contraction rate...

A-Level revision? It has to be CGP!

Published by CGP

Editors:
Charlotte Burrows, Ellen Burton, Daniel Fielding, Christopher Lindle, Emily Sheraton, Hayley Thompson.

Contributors:
Mark Ellingham, Emily Lucas, Bethan Parry, Megan Pollard, Duncan Wiles.

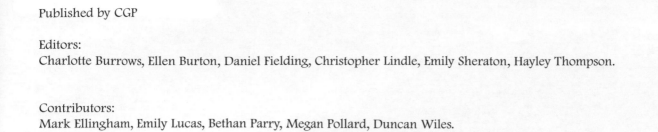

Graph on page 37 reprinted from Journal of Alzheimer's Disease 28, Bohrmann et al, Gantenerumab: A Novel Human Anti-Aβ Antibody Demonstrates Sustained Cerebral Amyloid-β Binding and Elicits Cell-Mediated Removal of Human Amyloid-β, pages 46–49, copyright 2012, with permission from IOS Press.

Graph on page 45 contains public sector information published by the Health and Safety Executive and licensed under the Open Government Licence.

Every effort has been made to locate copyright holders and obtain permission to reproduce sources. For those sources where it has been difficult to trace the originator of the work, we would be grateful for information. If any copyright holder would like us to make an amendment to the acknowledgements, please notify us and we will gladly update the book at the next reprint. Thank you.

ISBN: 978 1 78294 908 4

With thanks to Janet Cruse-Sawyer, Sarah Pattison, Rachael Rogers, Camilla Simson and Karen Wells for the proofreading.
With thanks to Ana Pungartnik for the copyright research.

Printed by Elanders Ltd, Newcastle upon Tyne

Based on the classic CGP style created by Richard Parsons.

# Contents

Use the tick boxes to check off the topics you've completed.


Exam Advice ........ 2

## Topic One — Biological Molecules

Biological Molecules — 1 ........ 3
Biological Molecules — 2 ........ 5
Biological Molecules — 3 ........ 9
More Biological Molecules ........ 13

## Topic Two — Cells

Cell Structure and Division — 1 ........ 16
Cell Structure and Division — 2 ........ 19
Cell Structure and Division — 3 ........ 22
Cell Membranes — 1 ........ 26
Cell Membranes — 2 ........ 29
Cells and the Immune System — 1 ........ 31
Cells and the Immune System — 2 ........ 35

## Topic Three — Exchange and Transport

Exchange and Transport Systems — 1 ........ 39
Exchange and Transport Systems — 2 ........ 43
More Exchange and Transport Systems — 1 ........ 46
More Exchange and Transport Systems — 2 ........ 50
More Exchange and Transport Systems — 3 ........ 53
More Exchange and Transport Systems — 4 ........ 56

## Topic Four — Genetic Information and Variation

DNA, RNA and Protein Synthesis ........ 59
Diversity, Classification and Variation — 1 ........ 63
Diversity, Classification and Variation — 2 ........ 66
Diversity, Classification and Variation — 3 ........ 70
Diversity, Classification and Variation — 4 ........ 73

Mixed Questions ........ 75

Answers ........ 81

# Exam Advice

Good exam technique can make a big difference to your marks, so make sure you read this stuff carefully.

## Get Familiar with the **Exam Structure**

If you're sitting the A-level in Biology rather than the AS, you'll be sitting a different set of exams to the ones described here. The exams will include the same types of questions though (plus a few extra).

For **AS Biology**, you'll be sitting **two papers**.

| | |
|---|---|
| **Paper 1** (topics 1-4, plus practical skills)<br>**1 hour 30 minutes** 75 marks **50%** of your AS | **Short** answer questions, plus a **10 mark comprehension** question. |
| **Paper 2** (topics 1-4, plus practical skills)<br>**1 hour 30 minutes** 75 marks **50%** of your AS | **Short** answer questions, plus **10 marks** of **extended response questions**. |

1) The **short** answer questions in Paper 1 and Paper 2 will test you on the **facts** you need to know, on whether you can **apply your knowledge** to unfamiliar contexts, and on your **practical skills**. There will also be a few **calculation** questions.
2) The **extended response** questions in Paper 2 require you to write a **longer answer** with a **logical structure**. E.g. you could be asked to describe the **steps** in a particular **process**.
3) For the **comprehension** question in Paper 1, you will be given a **passage** of information to read. You'll then need to answer the question parts that follow using both the information you've been given, and your own scientific knowledge.

## **Manage Your Time** Sensibly

1) The **number of marks** tells you roughly **how long** to spend on a question — you've got **just over a minute per mark** in each AS-level paper. So if you get stuck on a short question, it's sometimes worth **moving on** to another one, and then **coming back** to it if you've got time **at the end**.
2) Bear in mind, you might want to spend a **bit longer** per mark on the **extended response** and **comprehension** questions.

## **Command Words** Tell You **What You Need** to do in a Question

**Command words** are the bits of a question that tell you **what to do**. You'll find answering exam questions much easier if you understand exactly what they mean. Here are some of the **most common ones**:

| Command word | What to do |
|---|---|
| Give / Name / State | Give a brief **one or two word** answer, or a short sentence. |
| Describe | Write about what something's like. E.g. describe the structure of a cell. |
| Explain | **Give reasons** for something. |
| Suggest | Use your **scientific knowledge** to work out what the answer **might** be. |
| Calculate | Work out the **solution** to a mathematical problem. |
| Evaluate | Give arguments both **for and against** an issue, or the advantages and disadvantages of something. You should give an **overall judgement** too. |

Some questions will ask you to answer '**using the information/data provided**' — if so, you must **refer** to the information, data or figure you've been given or you won't get the marks. **Not all** of the questions will have command words either — instead they may just ask a '**which**' or '**what**' type of question.

# Biological Molecules — 1

There's a huge variety of life on Earth, but all organisms share the same few groups of carbon-based compounds. There might only be a few of these groups, but I've still managed to put plenty of exam-style questions together for you to have a go at. Best get to it — you can thank me later.

**1** **Figure 1** shows a polymer.

**Figure 1**

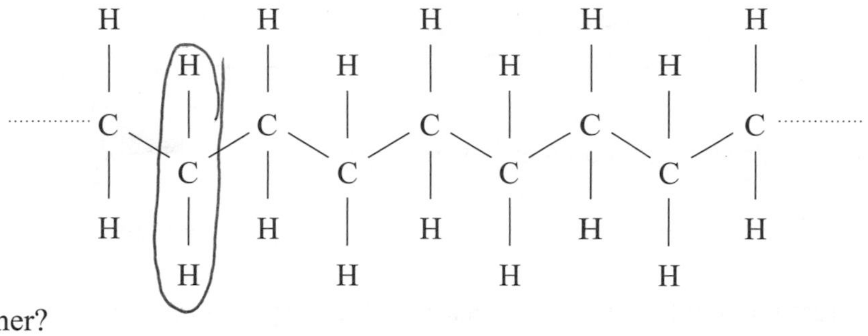

1.1 What is a polymer?

are large complex molecules composed of monmers joined together

**(1 mark)**

1.2 Draw a circle around a single monomer in **Figure 1**.

**(1 mark)**

1.3 Give **three** types of monomer found in biological molecules.

mono saccharides , amino asid ,

nucletides

**(1 mark)**

**2** **Figure 2** shows a reaction between two monomers that produces a disaccharide.

**Figure 2**

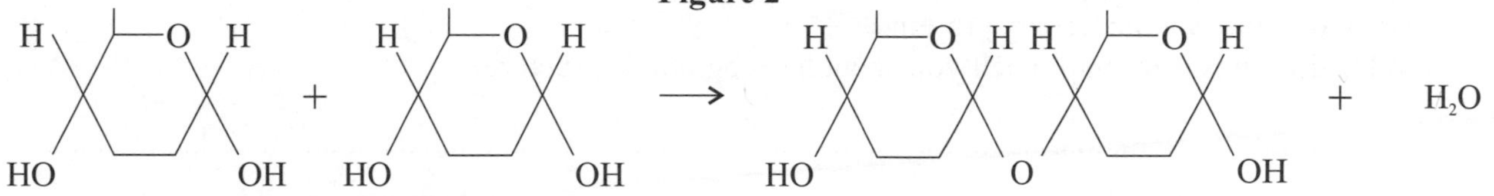

+ $H_2O$

2.1 Name the monomers shown in **Figure 2**.

Alfa glucose

**(1 mark)**

2.2 Name the disaccharide produced in **Figure 2**.

Maltose

**(1 mark)**

2.3 Disaccharides can be broken down.
Describe this reaction.

Water is used Hydrolysis reaction . Alfa glucose

**(3 marks)**

**3** Proteins have four levels of structure.

**Figure 3** shows part of the secondary structure of a protein.

**Figure 3**

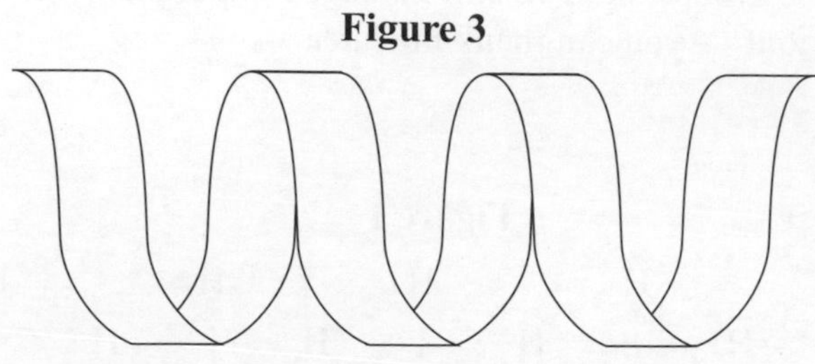

3.1 State which secondary structure is shown in **Figure 3**.

alfa helx

**(1 mark)**

3.2 Compare and contrast the bonding in the secondary and tertiary structures of a protein.

in Secondary structure there are only H-bonds but in terliary structures there are more bonds & there are H-bond & ionic bonds

**(2 marks)**

3.3 Explain why the tertiary structure of proteins is important for metabolic reactions.

because it form enzymes which build up them 3D shap in the terlary structure specialy the active site

**(3 marks)**

3.4 Haemoglobin is a quaternary protein.
What does this information tell you about haemoglobin's structure?

**(2 marks)**

Haemoglobin is the oxygen-carrying molecule in red blood cells.
At low pH, haemoglobin's ability to bind to oxygen is reduced.

3.5 Suggest why a low pH affects haemoglobin in this way.

**(2 marks)**

EXAM TIP

Take your time to really read the question — every word is carefully chosen. You need to look out for command words. The phrase "compare and contrast" means the examiner wants you to talk about the similarities and differences. It'd be really easy to forget to mention the differences here and just talk about the similarities, but you'd lose yourself marks that way.

Score

18

# Biological Molecules — 2

**1** Proteins are polymers of amino acids.

**Figure 1** shows the amino acid alanine.

**Figure 1**

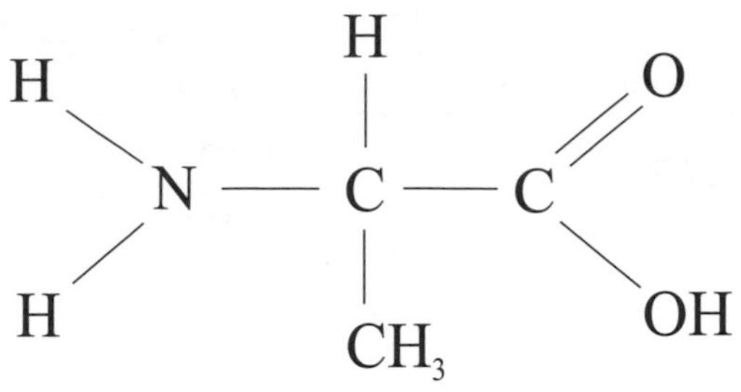

H
H O
N — C — C
H CH$_3$ OH

1.1 On **Figure 1**, circle and label the carboxyl group, the R group and the amino group.

**(3 marks)**

1.2 How is alanine different to the other 19 amino acids?

..........................................................................................................................................

**(1 mark)**

1.3 Draw a diagram of the dipeptide formed from the reaction between two molecules of alanine.
Label the peptide bond.

**(2 marks)**

1.4 Name the molecule required to break the peptide bond between two amino acids.

..........................................................................................................................................

**(1 mark)**

1.5 If this molecule alone is added to a dipeptide under neutral conditions in a laboratory, the peptide bond does not break down.
Explain why the bond is able to break down in the human body but not in the laboratory.

..........................................................................................................................................

..........................................................................................................................................

**(2 marks)**

**2** Three food samples (**A**, **B** and **C**), each containing carbohydrates, were tested using different techniques.

The results of these tests are shown in **Table 1**.

**Table 1**

| Sample | Test Results | | |
|---|---|---|---|
| | Test with iodine dissolved in potassium iodide solution | Test with Benedict's solution | Test with Benedict's solution (after heating with dilute hydrochloric acid) |
| A | Negative | Negative | Positive |
| B | Positive | Negative | Negative |
| C | Negative | Positive | Negative |

2.1 Describe how to carry out a Benedict's test and what would indicate a positive result.

..........................................................................................................................................

..........................................................................................................................................

..........................................................................................................................................

**(2 marks)**

The tests shown in **Table 1** allow the type of carbohydrate in each sample to be identified.

2.2 Using the information provided in **Table 1**, complete **Table 2** by placing a tick (✓) in the column that correctly identifies the type of carbohydrate present.

**Table 2**

| Sample | Type of carbohydrate present | | |
|---|---|---|---|
| | Reducing sugar | Non-reducing sugar | Starch |
| A | | | |
| B | | | |
| C | | | |

**(2 marks)**

Two more samples were tested and found to contain reducing sugars.

2.3 Describe how the amounts of reducing sugar in the two samples could be compared.

..........................................................................................................................................

..........................................................................................................................................

**(1 mark)**

The reducing sugar present in one of the samples was identified as lactose.

2.4 Name the **two** monomers that form a lactose disaccharide.

..........................................................................................................................................

**(1 mark)**

3 **Figure 2** shows a type of biological molecule.

**Figure 2**

```
                              H     H     H     H     H     H
                        O     |  H  |  H  |  H  |  H  |  H  |
             H          ||   /C\ | /C\ | /C\ | /C\ | /C\ | /C-H
             |      H-C-O-C     C     C     C     C     C  |
         H-C-O-C       |     H  |  H  |  H  |  H  |  H  |  H
             |                  H     H     H     H     H
             |
             |                H     H
             |          O     |  H  |  H  H           H
             |          ||   /C\ | /C\ | |  H  H  H  |
         H-C-O-C            | C   C=C   | /C\ | /C-H
             |              H  |  H  |   C   C  |  |
    O        |                 H     H   |  H  C  H
    ||       |                           H     |
R-O-P-O-C-H                                    H
    |   |
    O-  H
```

3.1 Name the type of molecule shown in **Figure 2**.

..........................................................................................................................................

**(1 mark)**

A droplet of these molecules was placed in water.
The molecules took the arrangement shown in **Figure 3**.

**Figure 3**

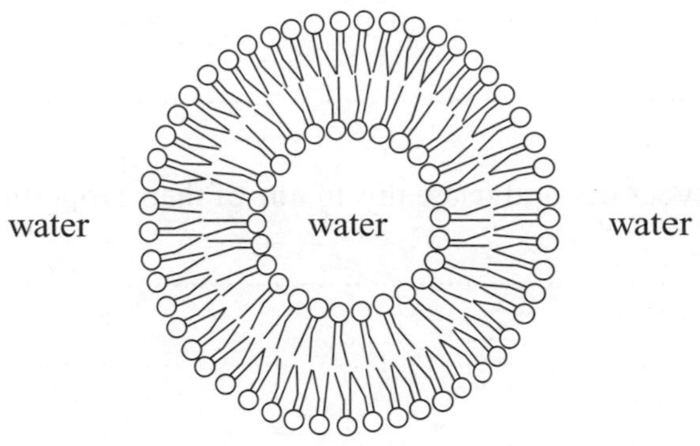


3.2 Explain why the molecules arranged themselves in this way.

..........................................................................................................................................

..........................................................................................................................................

..........................................................................................................................................

..........................................................................................................................................

**(3 marks)**

3.3 Describe **one** role that the molecules shown in **Figure 3** have in a cell.

..........................................................................................................................................

..........................................................................................................................................

..........................................................................................................................................

**(2 marks)**

4 **Figure 4** shows two different fatty acids.

**Figure 4**

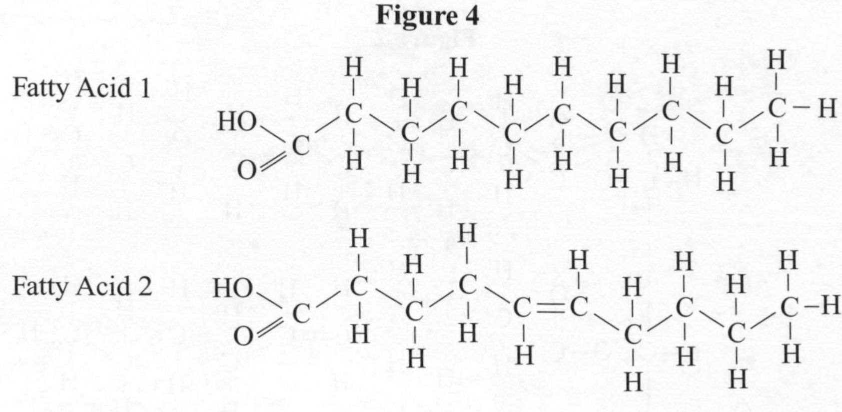


4.1 Explain the difference between these two fatty acids.

.................................................................................................................................

.................................................................................................................................

.................................................................................................................................

**(2 marks)**

Triglycerides contain fatty acids.

4.2 Describe how triglycerides are formed.

.................................................................................................................................

.................................................................................................................................

.................................................................................................................................

**(3 marks)**

4.3 Give **one** function of triglycerides and relate this to **one** of their properties.

.................................................................................................................................

.................................................................................................................................

**(2 marks)**

The emulsion test can be used to test for lipids.

4.4 Describe the emulsion test, including a positive result.

.................................................................................................................................

.................................................................................................................................

**(2 marks)**

4.5 An emulsion is droplets of one liquid suspended in another liquid.
Using this information, explain why lipids give a positive result in the emulsion test.

.................................................................................................................................

.................................................................................................................................

**(1 mark)**

You need to be really familiar with the structure of proteins, lipids and carbohydrates. You might get asked to identify a type of molecule or one of its groups from a diagram. Practise drawing these molecules out at home to help you visualise them — and don't be afraid to take a minute to quickly sketch out a molecule in your exam if it helps you to answer the question.

Score

31

# Biological Molecules — 3

**1** Glycogen, starch and cellulose are all polymers of glucose.

1.1 Explain how the structure of glycogen makes it well-suited to its function.

.....................................................................................................................................

.....................................................................................................................................

.....................................................................................................................................

**(2 marks)**

Starch is made of alpha-glucose molecules and cellulose is made of beta-glucose molecules.

1.2 Draw the structure of beta-glucose below and explain how it is different from that of alpha-glucose.

.....................................................................................................................................

.....................................................................................................................................

**(2 marks)**

1.3 The beta-glucose molecules allow cellulose to form long, straight chains with multiple hydrogen bonds between the chains. Explain how this makes cellulose well-suited to its function.

.....................................................................................................................................

.....................................................................................................................................

**(2 marks)**

Starch is a mixture of two polysaccharides of alpha-glucose, amylose and amylopectin.
The structures of amylose (**A**) and amylopectin (**B**) are shown in **Figure 1**.

**Figure 1**

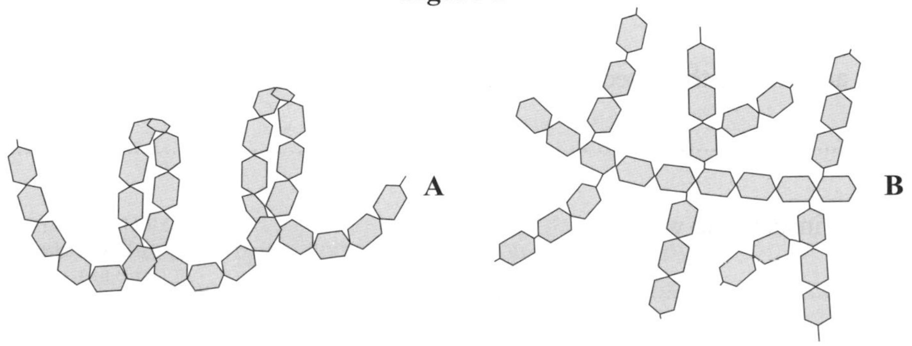

A

B

1.4 Different starches are made up of different proportions of amylose and amylopectin.
Using **Figure 1**, suggest **one** advantage and **one** disadvantage of using amylose to store excess glucose, rather than amylopectin.

Advantage: ..........................................................................................................................

Disadvantage: ......................................................................................................................

**(2 marks)**

The results of the student's first experiment are shown in **Figure 3**.

**Figure 3**

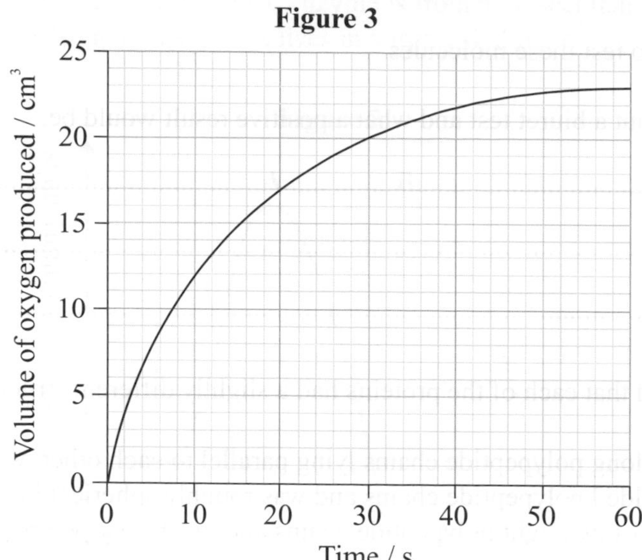


The student collected the oxygen in a measuring cylinder submerged in water.
The measuring cylinder measured to the nearest 1 $cm^3$.

4.2 Give the uncertainty of measurements associated with this measuring cylinder.

uncertainty = ...................................... $cm^3$
**(1 mark)**

4.3 Suggest **one** way that the student could have obtained more accurate results.

..........................................................................................................................................................
**(1 mark)**

4.4 Calculate the average rate of the reaction shown in **Figure 3** for the first 20 seconds.

rate = ...........................................
**(2 marks)**

4.5 Calculate the initial rate of the reaction shown in **Figure 3**.

To calculate the initial rate, you need to draw a tangent.

rate = ...........................................
**(1 mark)**

4.6 Sketch on the same axes the curve you would expect if the experiment were carried out with a higher enzyme concentration.

**(1 mark)**

Pen, pencil, ruler, calculator... Oh, that's just my shopping list for my exam. Sometimes examiners will ask you to draw, measure or calculate, so you need to make sure you've got all this stationery — a ruler that can measure in millimetres, a calculator, a pencil (for drawing graphs) and a pen with black ink. In fact, make sure you've got a couple of spare pens too.

Score

34

# More Biological Molecules

DNA, water and ions are essential for cell function in living organisms, and being able to answer questions about them is essential for your exams. This one might only be a short section, but make sure you give it a go.

**1** Inorganic ions play many important roles in organisms.

1.1 Give **one** role that sodium ions ($Na^+$) play in living cells.

..............................................................................................................................................

**(1 mark)**

1.2 Explain how the concentration of hydrogen ions ($H^+$) affects the internal environment of an organism.

..............................................................................................................................................

..............................................................................................................................................

**(2 marks)**

1.3 Suggest why nitrate ions ($NO_3^-$) are needed to make DNA.

..............................................................................................................................................

..............................................................................................................................................

**(2 marks)**

**2** Animals living in hot, dry climates have developed behaviours that help them keep cool.

Kangaroos have been observed licking saliva onto their forearms in hot weather.

2.1 Using your knowledge of the properties of water, explain why this behaviour helps the kangaroos to keep cool.

..............................................................................................................................................

..............................................................................................................................................

..............................................................................................................................................

..............................................................................................................................................

**(3 marks)**

Koalas have been observed to hug trees in hot weather.
This is thought to be because the trunks of trees are usually cooler than the surrounding air.

2.2 Tree trunks contain a lot of water.
Explain how this could contribute to the tree trunks being cooler than the surrounding air.

..............................................................................................................................................

..............................................................................................................................................

**(2 marks)**

2.3 Explain how water is able to flow up a tree trunk, from the roots to the leaves.

..............................................................................................................................................

..............................................................................................................................................

**(2 marks)**

**3** RNA carries genetic information from DNA to the ribosomes.

**Figure 1** shows part of the structure of an RNA molecule.

**Figure 1**

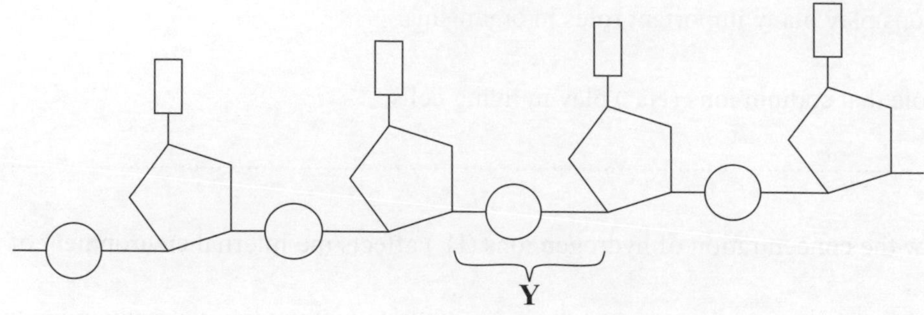


3.1 Name the bond labelled **Y** in **Figure 1**.

.................................................................................................................................................

**(1 mark)**

3.2 What type of reaction results in the formation of the bond labelled **Y**?

.................................................................................................................................................

**(1 mark)**

Some RNA molecules are capable of folding into structures known as stem-loops.
An example of a stem-loop structure is shown in **Figure 2**.

**Figure 2**

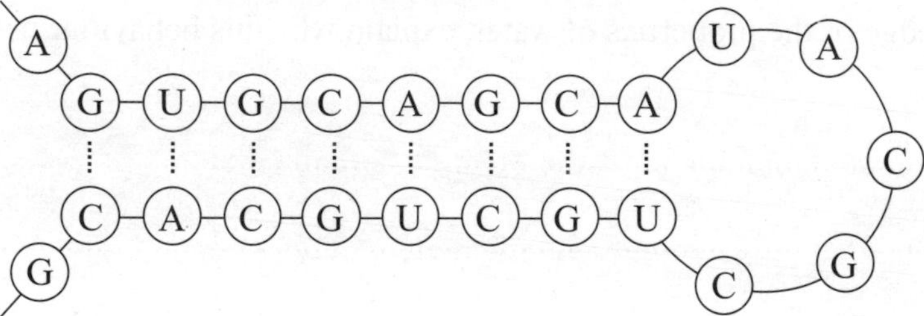


3.3 Looking at the sequence of the structure shown in **Figure 2**, explain how you can tell that this is part of an RNA molecule and not a DNA molecule.

.................................................................................................................................................

.................................................................................................................................................

**(1 mark)**

3.4 Using your knowledge of how DNA molecules can form a double helix, explain how the stem-loop structure shown in **Figure 2** is formed.

.................................................................................................................................................

.................................................................................................................................................

.................................................................................................................................................

.................................................................................................................................................

**(3 marks)**

**4** A scientist is investigating the role of enzymes in DNA replication.

4.1 Describe the roles that the enzymes DNA helicase and DNA polymerase play in DNA replication.

.............................................................................................................................

.............................................................................................................................

.............................................................................................................................

.............................................................................................................................

**(4 marks)**

The scientist mixes a bacterial DNA sample with the enzymes and substrates required for DNA replication. He does this in both the presence and the absence of ATP, and using active and inactive ATP hydrolase. He then measures the amount of DNA produced to determine whether DNA replication has taken place.

Some of the results of the investigation are shown in **Table 1**.

**Table 1**

| DNA replication enzymes | ATP hydrolase | ATP | Has DNA replication occurred? |
|---|---|---|---|
| Present | Active | Present | Yes |
| Present | Active | Absent | No |
| Present | Inactive | Present | No |
| Present | Inactive | Absent | No |

4.2 With reference to the structure of an ATP molecule, explain why ATP is known as a nucleotide derivative.

.............................................................................................................................

.............................................................................................................................

.............................................................................................................................

**(2 marks)**

4.3 Outline the reaction catalysed by ATP hydrolase.

.............................................................................................................................

.............................................................................................................................

**(2 marks)**

4.4 Describe and suggest an explanation for the results in **Table 1**.

.............................................................................................................................

.............................................................................................................................

.............................................................................................................................

.............................................................................................................................

.............................................................................................................................

**(3 marks)**

If you have to interpret the results of an unfamiliar experiment in the exam, don't panic — just make sure you read the method carefully. There'll always be some important information there that will help you understand the results. If you can take a minute to piece it together with everything you already know about those molecules, then you're sure to come out on top.

Score

29

# Cell Structure and Division — 1

All cells share some basic structural features, but there are plenty of differences you need to know about too. The structural differences between cell types are important for their particular functions and replication methods.

**1** A student investigated mitosis in plant tissue.

1.1 A 1 cm length was cut from the tip of an onion root.
This tip was incubated in dilute hydrochloric acid for 5 minutes at 60 °C.
It was then rinsed well with cold water and left to dry.
Describe how the student could have prepared a microscope slide to view the cells in this root tip.

..........................................................................................................................

..........................................................................................................................

..........................................................................................................................

..........................................................................................................................

**(4 marks)**

1.2 Give **two** safety precautions the student should have taken when preparing the slide.

1. ......................................................................................................................

2. ......................................................................................................................

**(2 marks)**

1.3 Explain why the student used the tip of the root for this investigation.

..........................................................................................................................

..........................................................................................................................

**(1 mark)**

The student's observations are shown in **Table 1**.

**Table 1**

| Type of cell | Number of cells |
|---|---|
| Dividing | 240 |
| Non-dividing | 80 |

1.4 Explain how the student was able to distinguish between dividing cells and non-dividing cells.

..........................................................................................................................

..........................................................................................................................

**(1 mark)**

1.5 Calculate the mitotic index of the root tip.

Mitotic index = ..............................................

**(2 marks)**

**2** Bacteria and viruses can cause disease when they infect humans.

*Staphylococcus aureus* can cause a range of illnesses in humans. The electron micrograph in **Figure 1** shows an intact *S. aureus* bacterium (right) and one undergoing lysis (left).

**Figure 1**

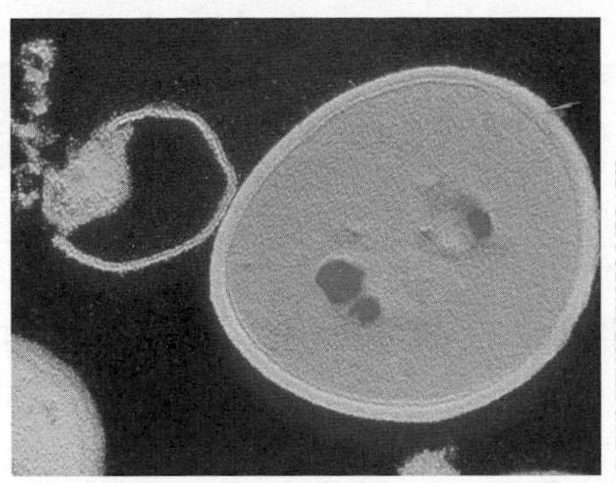


2.1 Give **one** reason why an electron microscope was used to view these cells rather than a light microscope.

.......................................................................................................................................

.......................................................................................................................................

**(2 marks)**

2.2 Name the type of electron microscope that was used to produce the micrograph seen in **Figure 1**. Give a reason for your answer.

.......................................................................................................................................

.......................................................................................................................................

**(2 marks)**

2.3 Give **two** ways in which you could distinguish between a prokaryotic cell and a eukaryotic cell in an electron micrograph.

1. .......................................................................................................................................

2. .......................................................................................................................................

**(2 marks)**

2.4 Penicillin is an antibiotic that can be used to treat infections of *Staphylococcus aureus*. The drugs cause cell lysis, as shown in **Figure 1**, by inhibiting cell wall synthesis. Explain why these drugs have no effect on human cells.

.......................................................................................................................................

.......................................................................................................................................

**(1 mark)**

2.5 The infection of human cells with West Nile Virus (WNV) can involve the cell surface receptor, $\alpha_v\beta_3$ integrin. Using your knowledge of the structure of viruses, suggest how a treatment that interferes with the function of $\alpha_v\beta_3$ integrin in human cells could prevent WNV replication.

.......................................................................................................................................

.......................................................................................................................................

.......................................................................................................................................

.......................................................................................................................................

**(3 marks)**

**3** Sperm cells are specialised for their function of delivering genetic material to the egg.

**Figure 2** shows the structure of a sperm cell.

**Figure 2**

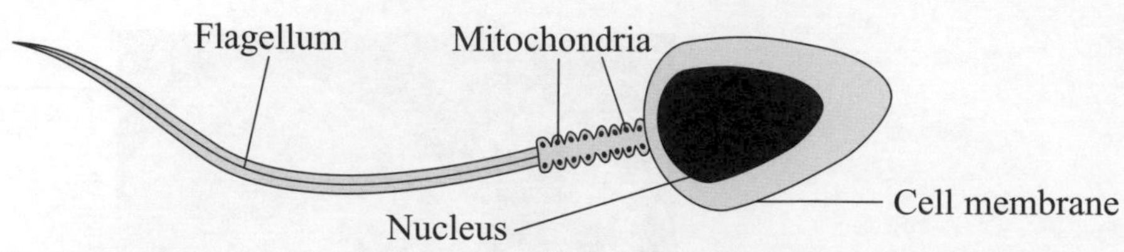


3.1 Using **Figure 2**, give **one** similarity and **one** difference between a sperm cell and a bacterium.

.......................................................................................................................................

.......................................................................................................................................

.......................................................................................................................................

.......................................................................................................................................

**(2 marks)**

3.2 Suggest why the mitochondria are located close to the sperm cell's flagellum.

.......................................................................................................................................

.......................................................................................................................................

**(1 mark)**

3.3 A scientist wanted to observe the mitochondria in a sample of sperm.

Which type of microscope should the scientist use to study the internal structures of the mitochondria? Explain your answer.

.......................................................................................................................................

.......................................................................................................................................

.......................................................................................................................................

**(2 marks)**

3.4 DNA is related to the function of a sperm cell and a mitotic body cell.
A mitotic body cell has many ribosomes, but a sperm cell does not.

With reference to the functions of these cells, explain why there is this difference in organelles.

.......................................................................................................................................

.......................................................................................................................................

.......................................................................................................................................

.......................................................................................................................................

**(3 marks)**

EXAM TIP

For questions on cell structure, you can be given a micrograph. It can be tricky to interpret these and to spot the different cell structures, but they are there. Trust me. To prepare yourself for the exam, make sure you learn what all the different cell structures look like.

Score

28

# Cell Structure and Division — 2

1 A team of scientists studied the organelles in **two** types of cell (**A** and **B**) taken from the body tissues of a eukaryotic organism.

**Table 1** shows the volume, as a percentage of the total cell volume, of **three** organelles.

**Table 1**

| Organelle | Percentage of total cell volume / % | |
|---|---|---|
| | Cell type **A** | Cell type **B** |
| Lysosomes | 4 | 1 |
| Rough endoplasmic reticulum | 8 | 16 |
| Nucleus | 7 | 7 |

1.1 Cell types **A** and **B** are both specialised cells. Define the term 'specialised cell'.

..........................................................................................................................................................

**(1 mark)**

1.2 The relative volume of the nucleus is the same in both types of cell. Suggest why.

..........................................................................................................................................................

..........................................................................................................................................................

**(1 mark)**

1.3 The role of one of the two cell types is to ingest invading pathogens, and the other is to secrete enzymes. Use **Table 1** to determine which of these two roles is carried out by cell type **A** and which is carried out by cell type **B**. Explain your answers.

..........................................................................................................................................................

..........................................................................................................................................................

..........................................................................................................................................................

..........................................................................................................................................................

..........................................................................................................................................................

**(4 marks)**

1.4 Two other organelles that can be found in eukaryotes are mitochondria and chloroplasts. Contrast the structure and function of these organelles to give **two** differences.

1. ..........................................................................................................................................................

..........................................................................................................................................................

2. ..........................................................................................................................................................

..........................................................................................................................................................

**(2 marks)**

**2** A student observed a sample of plant cells under a microscope.

2.1 Describe how to observe the cells in a prepared slide using a light microscope.

.............................................................................................................................................

.............................................................................................................................................

.............................................................................................................................................

.............................................................................................................................................

.............................................................................................................................................

.............................................................................................................................................

.............................................................................................................................................

**(5 marks)**

The student used an eyepiece graticule to calculate the size of some of the plant cells.
**Figure 1** shows the student's eyepiece graticule and stage micrometer.
The stage micrometer measures in millimetres.

**Figure 1**

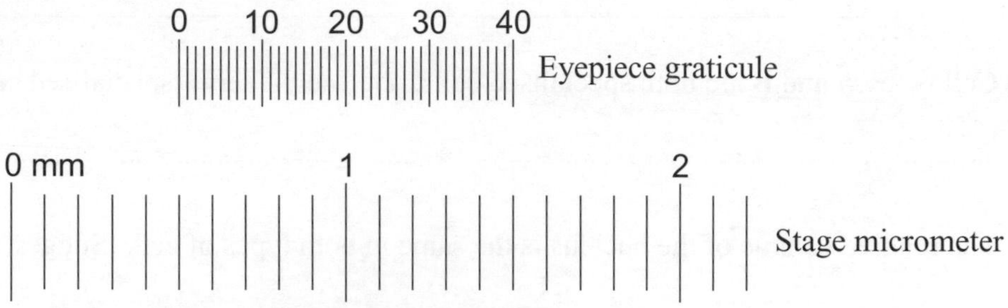

0 10 20 30 40 Eyepiece graticule

0 mm 1 2 Stage micrometer

2.2 Use **Figure 1** to calculate the size of **one** division on the student's eyepiece graticule, in micrometres.

........................................ µm
**(2 marks)**

2.3 The student increased the magnification, so he needed to recalibrate the eyepiece graticule.
Explain why the student needed to recalibrate the graticule.

.............................................................................................................................................

**(1 mark)**

Another student calculated the size of a cell from an image.
**Figure 2** shows the cell at × 100 magnification.

**Figure 2**

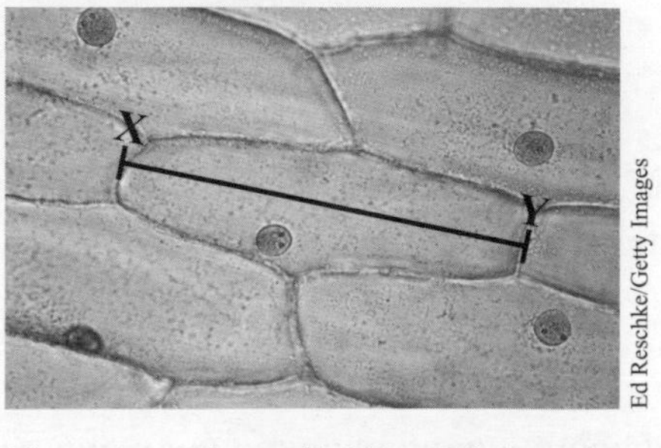

X Y

Ed Reschke/Getty Images

If you need to measure something in an exam, do it in millimetres. This'll make it easier to convert to micrometres (mm × 1000) or nanometres (µm × 1000).

2.4 Using **Figure 2**, calculate the real length of the cell (**X** to **Y**) in micrometres.

........................................ µm
**(2 marks)**

**3** Abnormal mitochondria have been found in diseased heart tissue, suggesting a link between mitochondria and heart disease. Scientists investigated this by producing a strain of mice with abnormal mitochondria. The abnormal mice developed symptoms of heart disease after one year.

3.1 Describe the main function of mitochondria.

.....................................................................................................................................

**(1 mark)**

3.2 Suggest why abnormal mitochondria might be problematic in heart tissue.

.....................................................................................................................................

.....................................................................................................................................

**(2 marks)**

**Figure 3** shows mitochondria in normal mice and the abnormal mice.

**Figure 3**

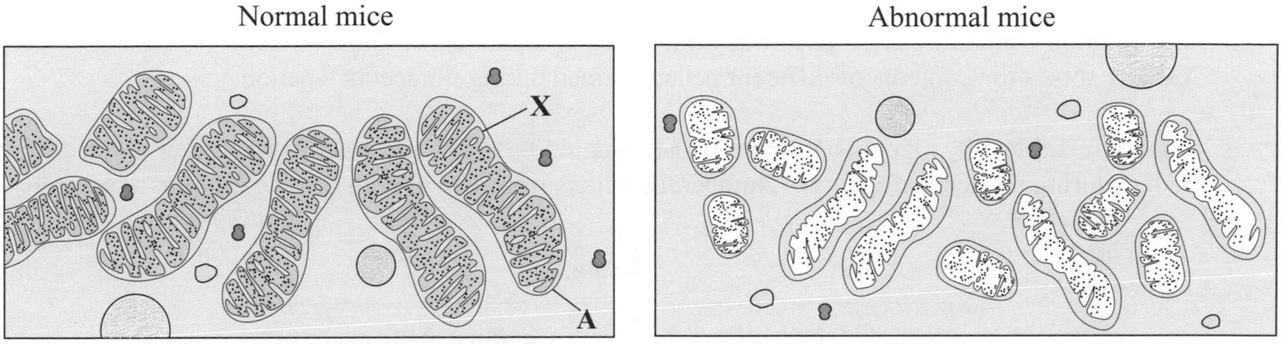

Normal mice

X

A

Abnormal mice

3.3 Name the part of the mitochondrion labelled **X** in **Figure 3**.

.....................................................................................................................................

**(1 mark)**

3.4 Describe **two** differences between the mitochondria found in the abnormal and normal mice.
Suggest how each difference may impair the function of mitochondria in the abnormal mice.

1. ..................................................................................................................................

.....................................................................................................................................

2. ..................................................................................................................................

.....................................................................................................................................

**(4 marks)**

3.5 The mitochondrion labelled **A** in **Figure 3** is about 1.5 μm in length.
Calculate the magnification of the image.

.............................................

**(2 marks)**

EXAM TIP

Maths always manages to worm its way in. You really need to make sure you learn some formulas, like the one for magnification (magnification = size of image ÷ size of real object). And make sure you *really* know them — you need to be confident rearranging them.

Score

28

# Cell Structure and Division — 3

**1** A scientist was separating organelles from a sample of plant cells.

1.1 Describe how the scientist could separate the organelles from other plant cell components.

..........

..........

..........

**(3 marks)**

1.2 After separation, the solution containing organelles was kept in an ice bath.
Explain why.

..........

**(1 mark)**

The solution containing organelles was centrifuged to separate them out.
**Table 1** shows the contents of different pellets formed during ultracentrifugation.

1.3 Complete **Table 1** by placing a number in the column to indicate the order of formation of the different pellets during ultracentrifugation. Number the pellets from **1** to **4**, with 1 being the first to separate out.

**Table 1**

| Contents of pellet | Sequence of separation |
|---|---|
| Mitochondria and chloroplasts | |
| Nuclei | |
| Ribosomes | |
| Endoplasmic reticulum | |

**(1 mark)**

1.4 A student commented on the results and suggested that the sample of plant cells were from a root.
Explain why the student is incorrect.

..........

..........

**(1 mark)**

1.5 Nuclear pore complexes (NPCs) control the passage of substances in and out of the nucleus.

In the scientist's study, cells from mutant plants with reduced NPC function were also centrifuged.
The cells from mutant plants produced a smaller pellet containing ribosomes, compared to cells from non-mutant plants. Explain why.

..........

..........

..........

..........

**(3 marks)**

**2** *Chlamydia trachomatis* is a bacteria that replicates within a host cell.

Once inside the host cell, *Chlamydia trachomatis* replicates normally. The replication of the bacteria causes the host cell to swell and eventually burst, releasing structures that can infect other cells.

2.1 Compare and contrast the replication of *C. trachomatis* with the replication of a virus.

.....................................................................................................................................

.....................................................................................................................................

.....................................................................................................................................

.....................................................................................................................................

.....................................................................................................................................

**(3 marks)**

*C. trachomatis* infections can be treated with azithromycin, a drug which inhibits ribosome function.

2.2 Explain the effect of this drug on bacterial growth.

.....................................................................................................................................

.....................................................................................................................................

.....................................................................................................................................

**(2 marks)**

2.3 Explain why azithromycin can't be used to treat viral infections.

.....................................................................................................................................

**(1 mark)**

A scientist compared the relative DNA content of a bacterial cell to its daughter cells, after the parent cell had divided to produce **two** daughter cells. The scientist's results are shown in **Table 2**.

**Table 2**

| Cell | DNA content relative to the parent cell |
|---|---|
| Daughter cell A | 1.4 |
| Daughter cell B | 0.8 |

2.4 Explain the results shown in **Table 2**.

.....................................................................................................................................

.....................................................................................................................................

.....................................................................................................................................

.....................................................................................................................................

**(2 marks)**

**3** A scientist was studying the stages of the cell cycle.

The scientist used a microscope to observe some cells undergoing mitosis.
**Figure 1** shows an image of **one** of these cells.

**Figure 1**

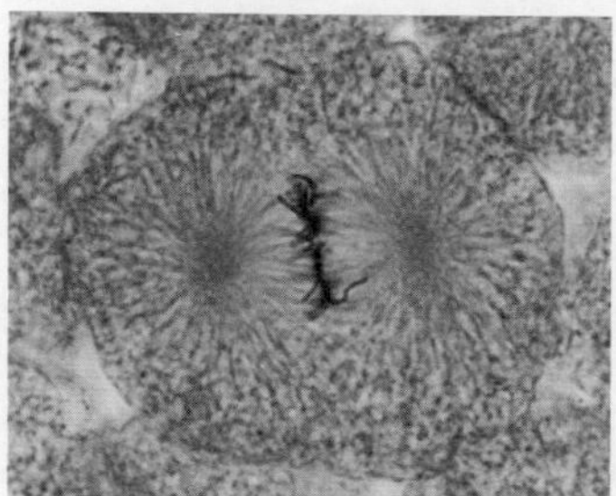

Ed Reschke/Getty Images

3.1 Name the stage of mitosis shown in **Figure 1** and explain your answer.

..........................................................................................................................................

..........................................................................................................................................

**(2 marks)**

Cyclins are proteins that play an important role in the cell cycle.
A scientist recorded the concentration of **two** cyclins (**E** and **B**) during part of the cell cycle shown in **Figure 2**. He also recorded the mass of DNA present in the parent cell during this period (also shown in **Figure 2**).

**Figure 2**

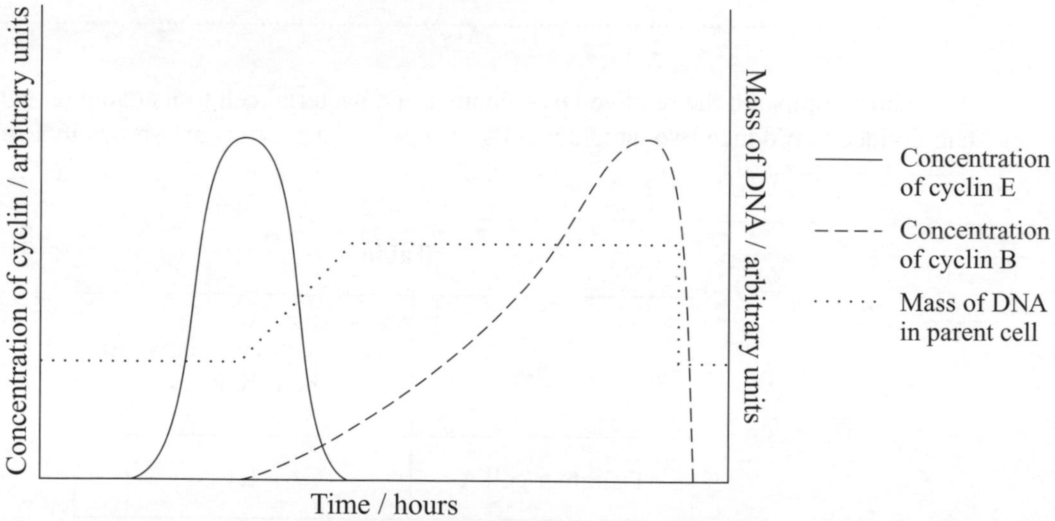

Concentration of cyclin / arbitrary units

Mass of DNA / arbitrary units

Time / hours

——— Concentration of cyclin E

– – – Concentration of cyclin B

······ Mass of DNA in parent cell

3.2 Using the results shown in **Figure 2**, suggest the functions of cyclins **E** and **B** in the cell cycle.

..........................................................................................................................................

..........................................................................................................................................

..........................................................................................................................................

..........................................................................................................................................

..........................................................................................................................................

..........................................................................................................................................

**(4 marks)**

**4** Chemotherapy is a type of drug treatment against cancer.

4.1 Chemotherapy can prevent the production of enzymes needed for DNA synthesis.
Using your knowledge of the cell cycle, explain why this prevents cancerous cells from dividing.

..........................................................................................................

..........................................................................................................

**(1 mark)**

4.2 A hair follicle is a sac at the root of a hair. Cells in the hair follicle divide frequently, causing hair growth. Suggest why non-cancerous cells in the hair follicle are more affected by chemotherapy than other non-cancerous body cells.

..........................................................................................................

..........................................................................................................

**(2 marks)**

4.3 A scientist took a sample of cancerous cells from a patient and calculated a mitotic index of 0.9.
The scientist observed a total number of 200 cells in the sample.
Calculate how many of the cells in this sample were undergoing mitosis at that time. Show your working.

..........................................

**(2 marks)**

Aurora kinases are important molecules for the formation of spindle fibres during mitosis.
Recent evidence suggests that an inhibitor of these molecules can be used to treat cancer.
The inhibitor causes shortened spindle fibres to form during prophase, as shown in **Figure 3**.

**Figure 3**

4.4 Using **Figure 3**, explain why these drugs could potentially be used as a method of treating cancer.

..........................................................................................................

..........................................................................................................

..........................................................................................................

..........................................................................................................

**(3 marks)**

EXAM TIP

Exam questions on the cell cycle often describe a way that the normal cycle is altered and ask you to explain what effect (if any) this has. As long as you know what usually happens during the different stages of the cell cycle, you should be able to work out what happens if something changes. It's important to be clued up about what happens during interphase and mitosis.

Score

31

# Cell Membranes — 1

Cell membranes may look simple through a microscope, but nothing's as simple as it first seems. In fact, they're actually pretty complex and really important for cells. These questions will make sure your knowledge is tip top.

**1** Cell membranes vary in structure due to the adaptation of specialised cells to their functions.

**Figure 1** models the arrangement of molecules in a typical cell membrane, observed from above.

**Figure 1**

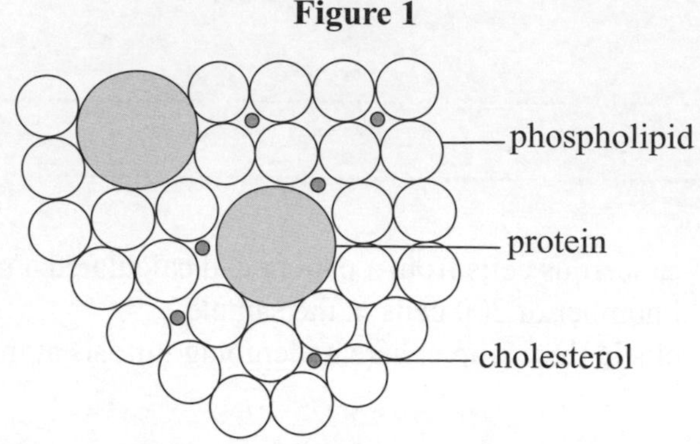


1.1 Describe the model illustrated in **Figure 1**.

..............................................................................................................................................

..............................................................................................................................................

**(2 marks)**

1.2 Explain the effect that a higher percentage of cholesterol would have on the model in **Figure 1**.

..............................................................................................................................................

..............................................................................................................................................

**(2 marks)**

Epithelial cells in the mammalian ileum absorb nutrients from a mammal's food.

1.3 Suggest and explain **two** ways in which the cell-surface membranes of these cells might be adapted to their function.

1. ..........................................................................................................................................

..............................................................................................................................................

2. ..........................................................................................................................................

..............................................................................................................................................

**(4 marks)**

The function of a neurone cell relies upon the rapid movement of cations across its cell membrane.

1.4 Suggest and explain an adaptation that you might expect to observe in the cell membrane of a neurone cell.

..............................................................................................................................................

..............................................................................................................................................

**(2 marks)**

**2** **Figure 2** shows part of the phospholipid bilayer in a cell-surface membrane.

**Figure 2**

Cell exterior — water potential = –0.5 kPa

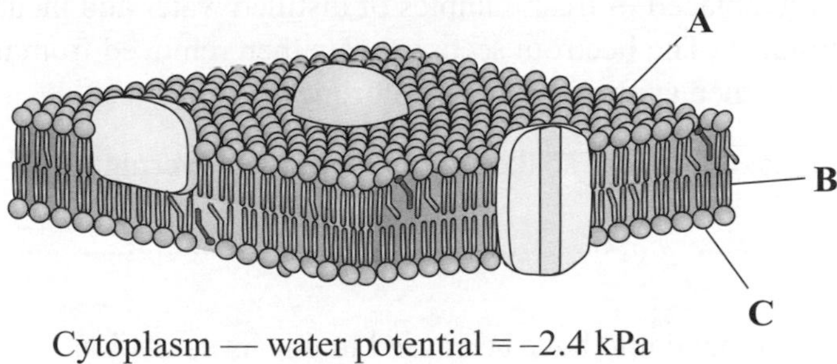


Cytoplasm — water potential = –2.4 kPa

2.1 Which letter (**A-C**) represents the hydrophobic part of the phospholipid bilayer?

.............................................................................................................................................

**(1 mark)**

2.2 When phospholipids come together to form a cell membrane, a bilayer structure is always formed. Explain why.

.............................................................................................................................................

.............................................................................................................................................

.............................................................................................................................................

.............................................................................................................................................

**(3 marks)**

2.3 Using the information in **Figure 2**, describe the direction of movement of water across the cell membrane. Give a reason for your answer.

.............................................................................................................................................

.............................................................................................................................................

.............................................................................................................................................

**(2 marks)**

**3** Explain how co-transport is used to transport sodium ions and glucose into cells in the mammalian ileum, across their cell membranes.

.............................................................................................................................................

.............................................................................................................................................

.............................................................................................................................................

.............................................................................................................................................

.............................................................................................................................................

.............................................................................................................................................

.............................................................................................................................................

**(5 marks)**

**4** Beetroot cells contain a vacuole. The vacuole contains red pigments called betalains, which are contained within the vacuole by a phospholipid membrane. A scientist wanted to investigate the effect of temperature on the permeability of this membrane.

Sections of beetroot were cut from the main plant and soaked in distilled water overnight. The cut sections were then placed in fresh samples of distilled water and incubated at different temperatures for 30 minutes. The beetroot sections were then removed from the water and discarded. Each sample of water was then analysed using a colorimeter.

4.1 Why were the cut sections of beetroot soaked in distilled water overnight?

.....................................................................................................................

**(1 mark)**

4.2 Suggest a negative control that could have been used in this investigation.

.....................................................................................................................

**(1 mark)**

**Table 1** illustrates the results that were obtained from the colorimetry analysis. The percentage absorbance illustrates the proportion of transmitted light at blue/green wavelengths that was absorbed by the pigments in the water.

**Table 1**

| Temperature / °C | Absorbance |
|---|---|
| 20 | 0.05 |
| 30 | 0.16 |
| 40 | 0.35 |
| 50 | 0.60 |
| 60 | 0.73 |

4.3 Use your knowledge of the structure of cell membranes to explain these results.

.....................................................................................................................

.....................................................................................................................

.....................................................................................................................

.....................................................................................................................

.....................................................................................................................

**(4 marks)**

4.4 A second investigation found that membrane permeability increased as the pH was decreased. Suggest an explanation for this.

.....................................................................................................................

.....................................................................................................................

.....................................................................................................................

**(3 marks)**

Examiners love a good practical question, so you'll need to brush up on terms like 'negative control'. When it comes to explaining results, be clear about what any table or graph is showing you — if the results for a colorimetry experiment show transmission of light rather than absorbance, the numbers will be the opposite way round to the ones above.

Score

30

# Cell Membranes — 2

1 Plants contain a mixture of solutes. Depending on the relative concentrations of solutes inside a plant cell and its environment, water will move into or out of the cell by osmosis.

Some students wanted to investigate the water potential of white potato cells. To do so they incubated samples of white potato in different concentrations of sucrose solution. The mass of each sample was measured before and after the incubation. The change in mass was then calculated. **Figure 1** shows a calibration curve of the results.

**Figure 1**

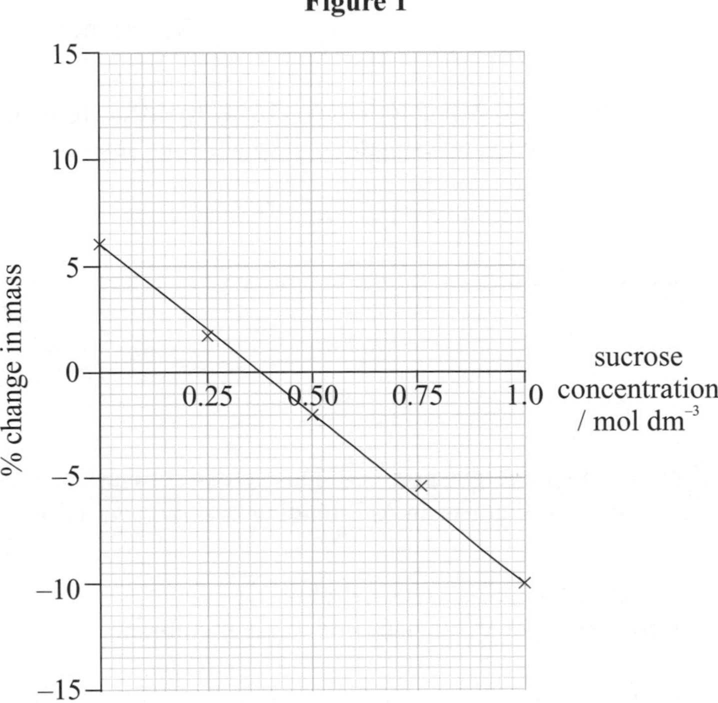


1.1 The students prepared the different concentrations of sucrose solution for their investigation using a stock solution of 1 mol $dm^{-3}$ sucrose solution and distilled water.
Complete **Table 1** to show the volumes of stock solution and water used to make up each concentration.

**Table 1**

| Concentration of sucrose solution to be made up / mol $dm^{-3}$ | Volume of 1 mol $dm^{-3}$ sucrose solution used / $cm^3$ | Volume of water used / $cm^3$ | Final volume of solution to be made up / $cm^3$ |
|---|---|---|---|
| 1 | 20 | 0 | 20 |
| 0.75 | 15 | | 20 |
| 0.5 | | | 20 |
| 0.25 | | | 20 |
| 0 | | | 20 |

**(2 marks)**

1.2 Give **two** control variables for this investigation.

1. ..........................................................................................

2. ..........................................................................................

**(2 marks)**

**Table 2** shows the relationship between sucrose concentration and water potential.

**Table 2**

| Sucrose concentration / mol dm$^{-3}$ | 0.1 | 0.2 | 0.3 | 0.4 | 0.5 | 0.6 | 0.7 | 0.8 | 0.9 | 1.0 |
|---|---|---|---|---|---|---|---|---|---|---|
| Water potential / kPa | –270 | –540 | –850 | –1130 | –1460 | –1810 | –2190 | –2590 | –3030 | –3530 |

1.3 Use **Table 2** and **Figure 1** to estimate the water potential of the potato tissue.
Show your working.

water potential = ................................ kPa
**(2 marks)**

1.4 Suggest how the water potential of sweet potato tissue is likely to differ from the water potential of the white potato tissue used in the students' investigation. Explain your answer.

..........................................................................................................................................

..........................................................................................................................................

..........................................................................................................................................
**(2 marks)**

**2** $Ca^{2+}$ ATPases are carrier proteins that transport $Ca^{2+}$ ions across cell-surface membranes. Each $Ca^{2+}$ ATPase has one subunit that has an ATP binding site and acts as an enzyme.

2.1 $Ca^{2+}$ ATPase spans the width of the cell-surface membrane.
The ATP binding site is always on the cytoplasm side of the membrane. Suggest why.

..........................................................................................................................................

..........................................................................................................................................
**(1 mark)**

2.2 Suggest and explain why $Ca^{2+}$ ATPase has a subunit that acts as an enzyme.

..........................................................................................................................................

..........................................................................................................................................

..........................................................................................................................................
**(2 marks)**

2.3 Explain why $Ca^{2+}$ ions are always transported across cell-surface membranes via carrier or channel proteins.

..........................................................................................................................................

..........................................................................................................................................
**(2 marks)**

EXAM TIP

'Estimate' means you need to give an approximate value rather than calculate an exact answer. It needs to be a sensible estimate though, not just a stab in the dark guess, so you need to think about the best method to use to obtain your estimate.

Score

13

# Cells and the Immune System — 1

Not all cells are as nice as the ones you've just seen — some are out to cause trouble. The following questions are all about disease and the immune response. I know, your primary response is going to want you to turn away from this page, but make sure you stick at it. You want to get those memory cells activated, ready for your exam.

1 **Figure 1** shows an antibody.

**Figure 1**

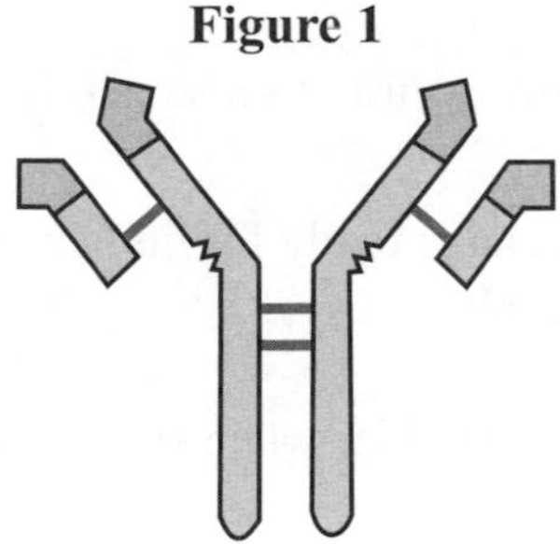

1.1 What is an antibody?

**(1 mark)**

1.2 Name a type of cell that produces antibodies.

**(1 mark)**

1.3 Explain how the structure of the antibody shown in **Figure 1** makes it adapted to its function.

**(3 marks)**

Some antibodies have a more complex structure, made up of several monomers joined together. This is shown in **Figure 2**.

**Figure 2**

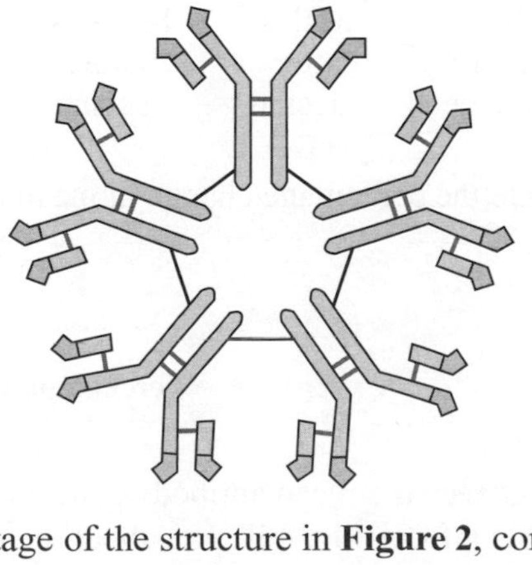

1.4 Suggest and explain **one** advantage of the structure in **Figure 2**, compared to that in **Figure 1**.

**(2 marks)**

1.5 Some cells can produce antibodies at a rate of 2000 molecules per second.
Calculate how many antibodies would be produced by one of these cells in one hour.
Give your answer in standard form.

number of antibodies = ..........................................

**(2 marks)**

**2** Scientists are developing a vaccine against a viral disease that is often fatal in young children.

The vaccine has been tested on animals and is ready for human trials.
Initially, the vaccine is being tested on adults.

2.1 Suggest **two** factors the scientists should consider when selecting adult volunteers for this trial.

1. ..........................................................................................................................................

2. ..........................................................................................................................................

**(2 marks)**

Scientists conducting the trial compared the mean antibody concentration in males and females before and after the vaccine was administered. The results are shown in **Figure 3**.

**Figure 3**

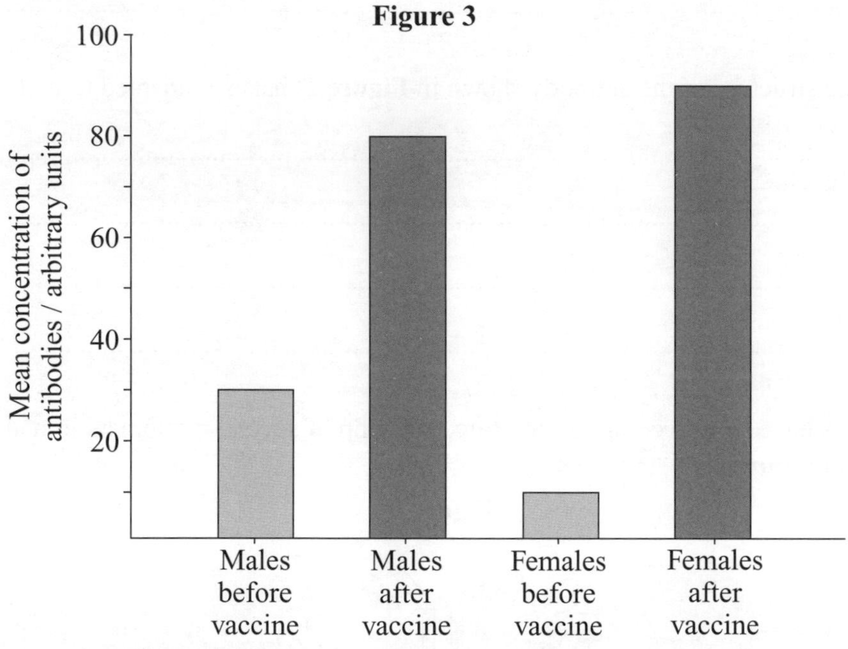


2.2 Using the data in **Figure 3**, calculate the percentage change in mean antibody concentration for females after they received the vaccine.

percentage change = ..........................................%

**(1 mark)**

2.3 Statistical tests on the difference between the mean antibody concentration in males and females showed a result of $P > 0.05$. Explain what this information tells you about the results.

..........................................................................................................................................

..........................................................................................................................................

**(2 marks)**

The scientists are aiming to protect all children who are vulnerable to this disease by 2040.

2.4 Explain why it is possible to protect all children in a population without vaccinating them all.

.............................................................................................................................................

.............................................................................................................................................

**(2 marks)**

Vaccination programmes are not always completely effective.
One possible cause for this lack of success is antigen variability.

2.5 Explain how antigen variability could prevent a vaccination programme from being entirely successful.

.............................................................................................................................................

.............................................................................................................................................

.............................................................................................................................................

**(3 marks)**

**3** **Figure 4** shows the structure of the human immunodeficiency virus (HIV).

**Figure 4**

3.1 On **Figure 4**, name and label the part of the virus which allows it to gain access to a host cell.

**(1 mark)**

3.2 HIV can only infect cells that express the CD4 cell-surface receptor, such as T-cells. Explain why.

.............................................................................................................................................

.............................................................................................................................................

.............................................................................................................................................

**(3 marks)**

HTLV-I is another virus that infects T-cells. It has the same structure as HIV and replicates the same way. The HTLV-I genetic material contains a gene called Tax. When T-cells express the Tax protein, they begin to divide uncontrollably.

3.3 Using this information, explain how a T-cell begins to express the Tax protein once the HTLV-I genetic material has gained access to the cell.

.............................................................................................................................................

.............................................................................................................................................

.............................................................................................................................................

.............................................................................................................................................

**(4 marks)**

**4** Leishmaniasis is a parasitic disease spread through the bites of sandflies.
**Figure 5** shows a method used for detecting the presence of *Leishmania* parasites in the blood.

**Figure 5**

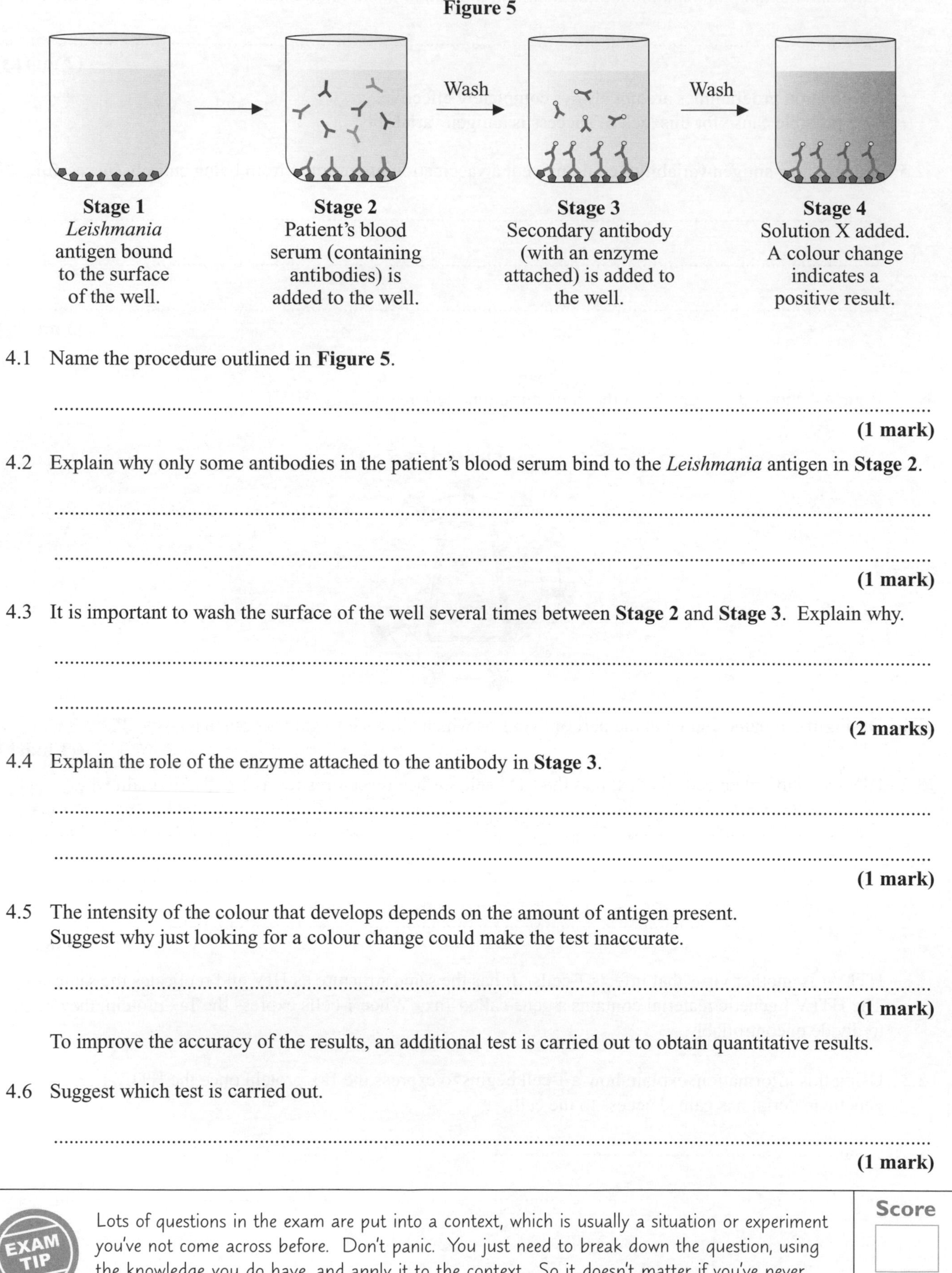


**Stage 1** *Leishmania* antigen bound to the surface of the well.

**Stage 2** Patient's blood serum (containing antibodies) is added to the well.

**Stage 3** Secondary antibody (with an enzyme attached) is added to the well.

**Stage 4** Solution X added. A colour change indicates a positive result.

4.1 Name the procedure outlined in **Figure 5**.

...........................................................................................................

**(1 mark)**

4.2 Explain why only some antibodies in the patient's blood serum bind to the *Leishmania* antigen in **Stage 2**.

...........................................................................................................

...........................................................................................................

**(1 mark)**

4.3 It is important to wash the surface of the well several times between **Stage 2** and **Stage 3**. Explain why.

...........................................................................................................

...........................................................................................................

**(2 marks)**

4.4 Explain the role of the enzyme attached to the antibody in **Stage 3**.

...........................................................................................................

...........................................................................................................

**(1 mark)**

4.5 The intensity of the colour that develops depends on the amount of antigen present.
Suggest why just looking for a colour change could make the test inaccurate.

...........................................................................................................

**(1 mark)**

To improve the accuracy of the results, an additional test is carried out to obtain quantitative results.

4.6 Suggest which test is carried out.

...........................................................................................................

**(1 mark)**

EXAM TIP

Lots of questions in the exam are put into a context, which is usually a situation or experiment you've not come across before. Don't panic. You just need to break down the question, using the knowledge you do have, and apply it to the context. So it doesn't matter if you've never heard of Leishmaniasis before, just use what you know about how monoclonal antibodies work.

Score

34

# Cells and the Immune System — 2

1 **Figure 1** shows the primary immune response following a bacterial infection.

**Figure 1**

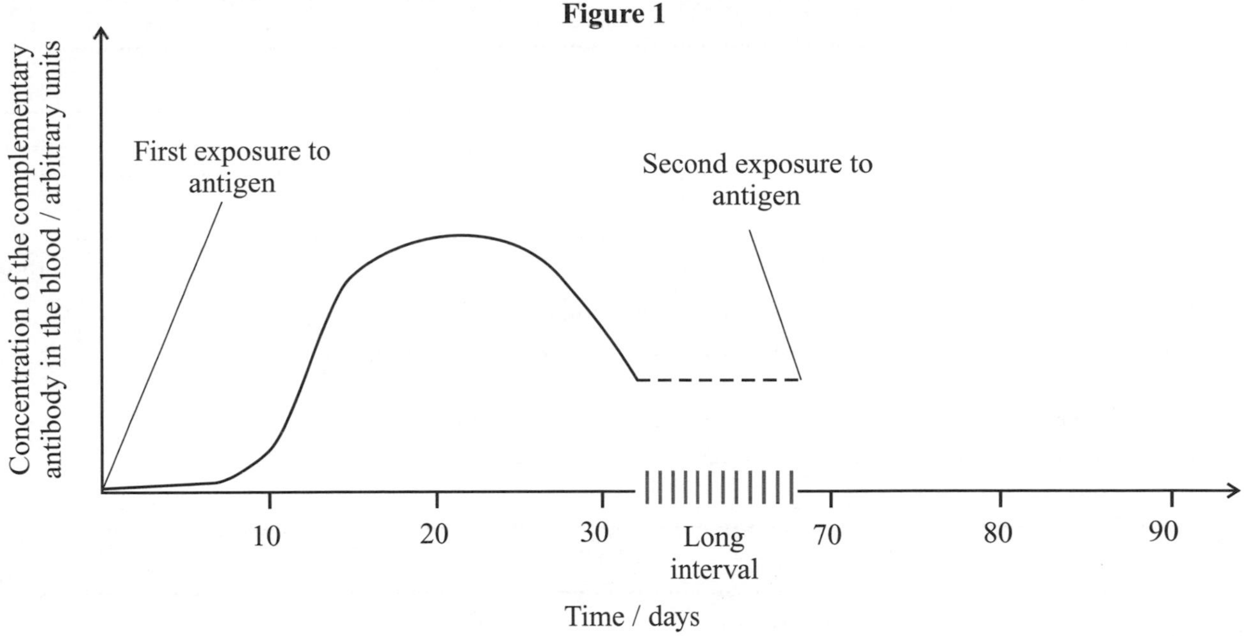


1.1 On **Figure 1**, sketch a line to represent the secondary immune response.

**(1 mark)**

1.2 Explain the shape of the curve for the primary immune response.

..........

..........

..........

..........

..........

..........

**(4 marks)**

2 Group B streptococcus (GBS) is a bacterium that can be carried, without harm, in a healthy human body. However, if a newborn baby becomes infected with GBS, it can lead to meningitis or other serious diseases.

GBS is typically passed on from a carrier mother to her baby during birth. Scientists are currently working to develop a vaccine against GBS, which will be given to pregnant women.

2.1 Suggest why a pregnant woman would be vaccinated against GBS when she is not at risk from infection.

..........

..........

**(1 mark)**

2.2 Describe how a vaccine could lead to immunity against a GBS infection.

.............................................................................................................

.............................................................................................................

.............................................................................................................

.............................................................................................................

.............................................................................................................

.............................................................................................................

.............................................................................................................

**(5 marks)**

When a baby breastfeeds, it receives some of its mother's antibodies.
This gives the baby immunity against the diseases its mother is immune to.

2.3 Describe **two** differences between the immunity obtained from breastfeeding with the immunity obtained from a vaccine.

1. .............................................................................................................

.............................................................................................................

2. .............................................................................................................

.............................................................................................................

**(2 marks)**

Meningitis occurs when the protective layers around the brain and spinal cord become infected.
It can be caused by bacteria, such as GBS, or certain viruses.

2.4 Meningitis caused by GBS bacteria can be treated with the antibiotic cefotaxime.
Cefotaxime intereferes with cell wall synthesis.
Using this information, explain why viral meningitis cannot be treated with cefotaxime.

.............................................................................................................

.............................................................................................................

**(1 mark)**

**3** Alzheimer's disease is a brain disorder characterised by symptoms such as memory loss and confusion. Scientists think that Alzheimer's disease may be the result of structures called amyloid plaques developing in the brain. Several monoclonal antibodies are being trialled as drugs to treat those diagnosed with Alzheimer's disease. One such drug, gantenerumab, is a monoclonal antibody that targets a protein called beta-amyloid, which is the main component of amyloid plaques.

3.1 Using your knowledge of the immune response, suggest how a monoclonal antibody that targets beta-amyloid might work to destroy plaques.

.............................................................................................................

.............................................................................................................

.............................................................................................................

**(2 marks)**

A group of scientists investigated how well gantenerumab cleared beta-amyloid plaques in the hippocampus area of mice brains. Some of their results are shown in **Figure 2**.

**Figure 2**

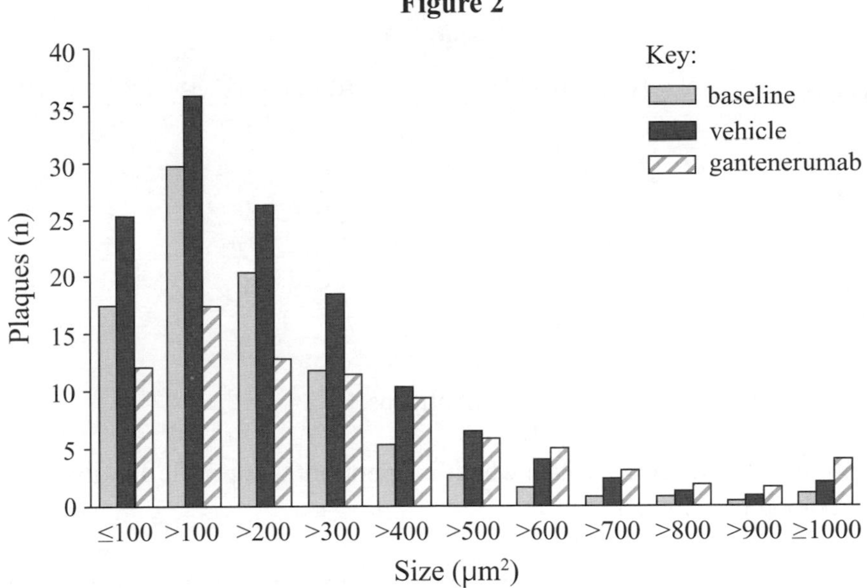


- The baseline data in **Figure 2** shows the size and number of plaques in untreated mice at the start of the investigation.
- The vehicle data shows the size and number of plaques in mice treated only with the vehicle used to deliver the gantenerumab and not with the drug itself.
- Treatment with both the vehicle and gantenerumab lasted 5 months.
  Results were recorded at the end of this time period.

3.2 Explain why some mice were treated with the vehicle only.

.....................................................................................................................................

.....................................................................................................................................

.....................................................................................................................................

**(2 marks)**

3.3 Give **one** conclusion that can be drawn from the results shown in **Figure 2**.

.....................................................................................................................................

.....................................................................................................................................

**(1 mark)**

3.4 A student looking at the data in **Figure 2** concluded that gantenerumab will be a useful treatment for Alzheimer's disease in humans.

Explain why this is not a valid conclusion.

.....................................................................................................................................

.....................................................................................................................................

.....................................................................................................................................

.....................................................................................................................................

.....................................................................................................................................

.....................................................................................................................................

**(4 marks)**

**4** **Figure 3** shows a simplified model of the different antigens present on red blood cells from different blood types.

**Figure 3**

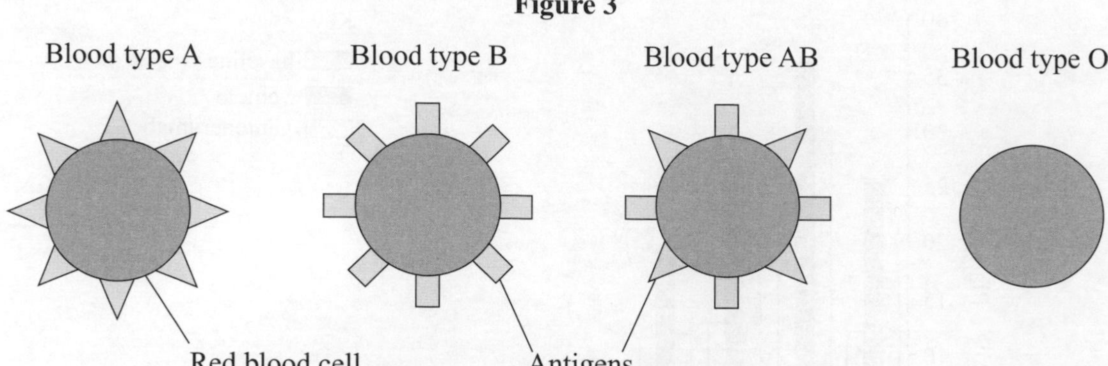


4.1 Use the information in **Figure 3** to explain why it is important that people are given the correct blood type when receiving a blood transfusion.

..........................................................................................................................

..........................................................................................................................

..........................................................................................................................

**(3 marks)**

4.2 Describe the sequence of events that would occur if **blood type B** was given to someone with **blood type A**.

..........................................................................................................................

..........................................................................................................................

..........................................................................................................................

..........................................................................................................................

..........................................................................................................................

..........................................................................................................................

..........................................................................................................................

**(6 marks)**

4.3 Explain why anyone can receive **type O** blood.

..........................................................................................................................

..........................................................................................................................

**(1 mark)**

4.4 Monoclonal antibodies can be used to determine a person's blood type. Suggest how.

..........................................................................................................................

..........................................................................................................................

**(2 marks)**

It's easy to get so bogged down trying to learn all the facts that you forget about practical skills — make sure you don't. Examiners love to bring bits from practical skills into questions to get you thinking outside the box. Make sure you know about things like experimental design, drawing conclusions, and validity, and that you can apply them to real-world examples.

Score

35

# Exchange and Transport Systems — 1

If you read 'Exchange and Transport Systems' and got excited about answering questions on the rail network, prepare to be disappointed. If you read 'Exchange and Transport Systems' and got excited about answering questions on how gases are exchanged in fish, insects, plants and humans... well, it's your lucky day.

1 **Figure 1** shows a gill filament of a fish.

**Figure 1**

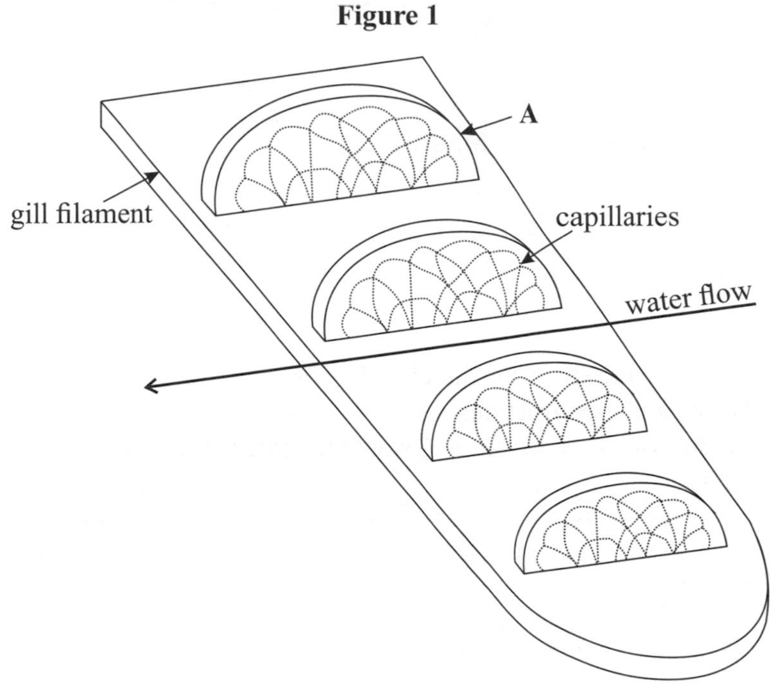


1.1 Name structure **A** on **Figure 1.**

..................................................................................................................................................

**(1 mark)**

1.2 Draw an arrow on structure **A** to show the direction of blood flow.

**(1 mark)**

1.3 Label structure **A** to show where the highest and lowest concentrations of oxygen are found in the blood.

**(1 mark)**

1.4 Explain **one** way in which the structure of the gill filament is adapted to its function.

..................................................................................................................................................

..................................................................................................................................................

..................................................................................................................................................

**(2 marks)**

2 A student dissected a grasshopper. As part of the dissection, she removed a piece of the grasshopper's exoskeleton.

2.1 Suggest a tool that the student could have used to cut through the exoskeleton.

..................................................................................................................................................

**(1 mark)**

**Figure 2** shows a diagram of the grasshopper's gas exchange system.

**Figure 2**

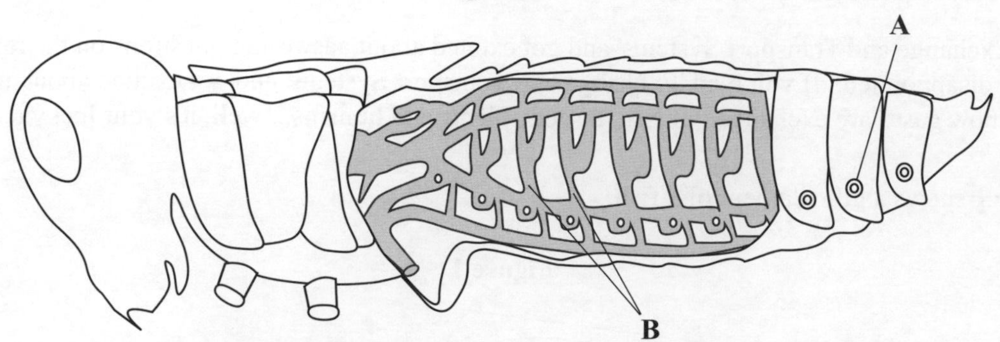


2.2 Identify the structures labelled **A** and **B** in **Figure 2**.

**A** ..........................................................................................................................................................

**B** ..........................................................................................................................................................

**(2 marks)**

2.3 The student wants to examine the structures labelled **B** more closely, with the use of a temporary mount. A stain is **not** needed to view these structures.
Using this information, describe how the student would prepare the mount.

..........................................................................................................................................................

..........................................................................................................................................................

..........................................................................................................................................................

..........................................................................................................................................................

**(3 marks)**

2.4 In insects, the need for efficient gas exchange can conflict with the need to limit water loss.
Give **two** ways that the grasshopper is adapted to limit water loss.

1. ..........................................................................................................................................................

2. ..........................................................................................................................................................

**(2 marks)**

**3** A student investigated the stomatal density of a non-xerophytic plant's leaves. She studied ten samples of lower epidermis under a microscope. The samples were taken from different leaves of the same plant.

**Table 1** shows the number of stomata the student counted within the microscope's field of view for each sample. The field of view measured 0.025 $mm^2$ in each case.

**Table 1**

| | Sample | | | | | | | | | |
|---|---|---|---|---|---|---|---|---|---|---|
| | 1 | 2 | 3 | 4 | 5 | 6 | 7 | 8 | 9 | 10 |
| Number of stomata | 5 | 6 | 7 | 4 | 3 | 8 | 5 | 5 | 3 | 4 |

3.1 Using **Table 1** and the information provided, estimate the number of stomata you would expect to find on a leaf with a surface area of 150 $mm^2$. Show your working.

Number of stomata: ..............................................

**(2 marks)**

3.2 Give **two** reasons why your answer to question **3.1** might not be an accurate estimate of the number of stomata present on the leaf.

1. ....................................................................................................

2. ....................................................................................................

**(2 marks)**

3.3 Name the cells that are the site of gas exchange in a leaf.

....................................................................................................

**(1 mark)**

**Figure 3** shows an electron micrograph image of part of a xerophyte leaf.

**Figure 3**

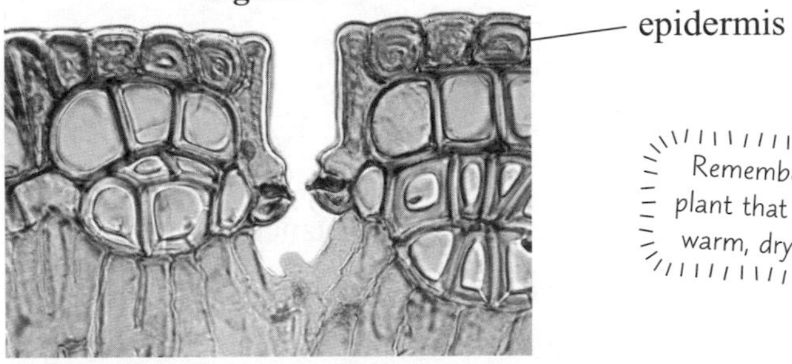

DR KEITH WHEELER/SCIENCE PHOTO LIBRARY

Remember, a xerophyte is a plant that is adapted to life in warm, dry or windy habitats.

3.4 Describe and explain the xerophytic adaptation shown in **Figure 3**.

....................................................................................................

....................................................................................................

....................................................................................................

....................................................................................................

**(3 marks)**

**4** *Lepus capensis* and *Lepus othus* are two species of hare.
*Lepus othus* has relatively short ears compared to *Lepus capensis*.

4.1 Which of these two hare species would you expect to find in Alaska, where the climate is cold? Explain your answer.

....................................................................................................

....................................................................................................

....................................................................................................

....................................................................................................

**(3 marks)**

4.2 Alaskan hares are hunted by larger mammals, such as polar bears. Explain how you would expect the metabolic rate of an Alaskan hare to differ from the metabolic rate of a polar bear.

....................................................................................................

....................................................................................................

....................................................................................................

....................................................................................................

**(3 marks)**

5 Sharks exchange oxygen across their gill lamellae using a counter-current gas exchange system. **Figure 4** shows how the relative oxygen concentration of water changes with distance along a shark's lamella.

**Figure 4**

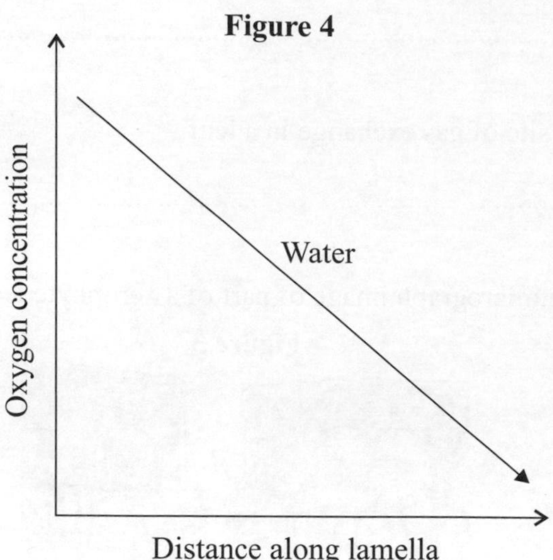


5.1 On **Figure 4**, sketch the relative oxygen concentration of the blood flowing through the lamella.

**(1 mark)**

**Figure 5** shows how the relative oxygen concentrations of water and blood would change with distance along a shark's lamella if gas exchange took place via a parallel flow system.

**Figure 5**

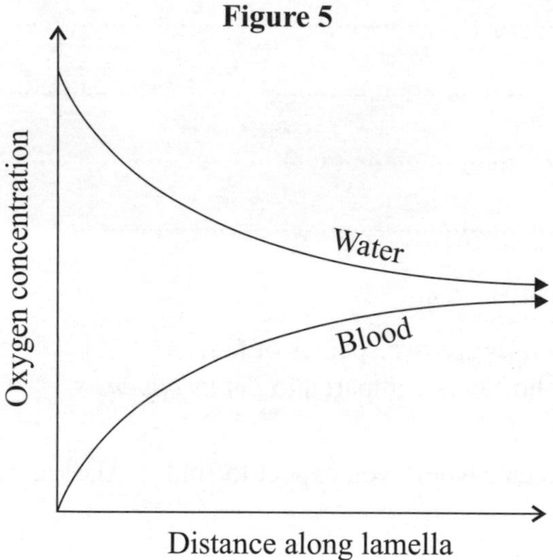


5.2 Use **Figure 5** to explain why a parallel flow gas exchange system would be less efficient than a counter-current gas exchange system.

..........................................................................................................................................

..........................................................................................................................................

..........................................................................................................................................

..........................................................................................................................................

..........................................................................................................................................

**(3 marks)**

Make sure your working is clear in calculation questions that are worth multiple marks. Even if you get the final answer wrong, you could pick up some marks from your working — but only if the marker can tell what you were trying to do and where you got your numbers from.

Score

31

# Exchange and Transport Systems — 2

**1** Bacterium **A** has a surface area to volume ratio of 5 : 1. Bacterium **B** has a surface area to volume ratio of 84 : 22. Bacterium **C** has a surface area of 15.75 $\mu m^2$ and a volume of 3.5 $\mu m^3$.

Use the information above to determine which **one** of the bacteria (**A**, **B** or **C**) is likely to be able to carry out gas exchange at the fastest rate. Show your working.

Bacterium: ..........................

**(2 marks)**

**2** Intrapulmonary pressure is the pressure inside the lungs.
**Figure 1** shows how intrapulmonary pressure changes during breathing.

**Figure 1**

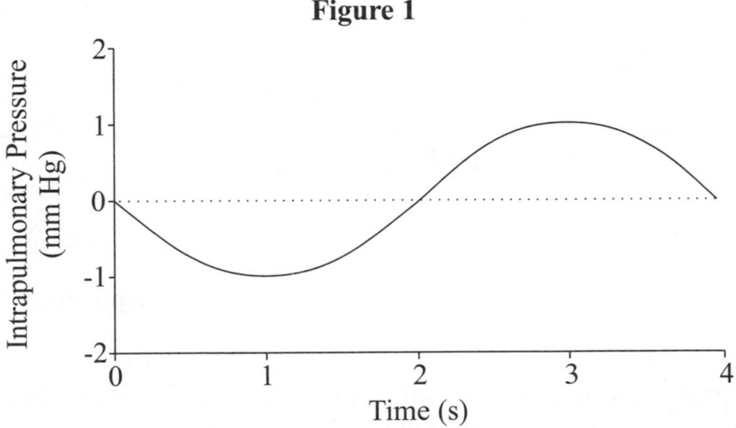


2.1 Name **two** muscles that contract when a person inspires.

1. ..........................................................................................

2. ..........................................................................................

**(2 marks)**

2.2 State the time period in **Figure 1** during which air is being taken into the lungs.
Explain your answer.

..........................................................................................

..........................................................................................

..........................................................................................

**(3 marks)**

2.3 State the time in **Figure 1** at which the lung volume is at its smallest.

..........................................................................................

**(1 mark)**

**3** Emphysema is a lung disease that leads to the breakdown of the alveoli walls.

3.1 Give **two** ways that healthy alveoli are adapted for gas exchange.

1. ..............................................................................................................................

..............................................................................................................................

2. ..............................................................................................................................

..............................................................................................................................

**(2 marks)**

Flow-volume loops show air flow during expiration and inspiration, plotted against the volume of air in the lungs. **Figure 2** shows a flow-volume loop for a healthy person and one for a patient with emphysema.

**Figure 2**

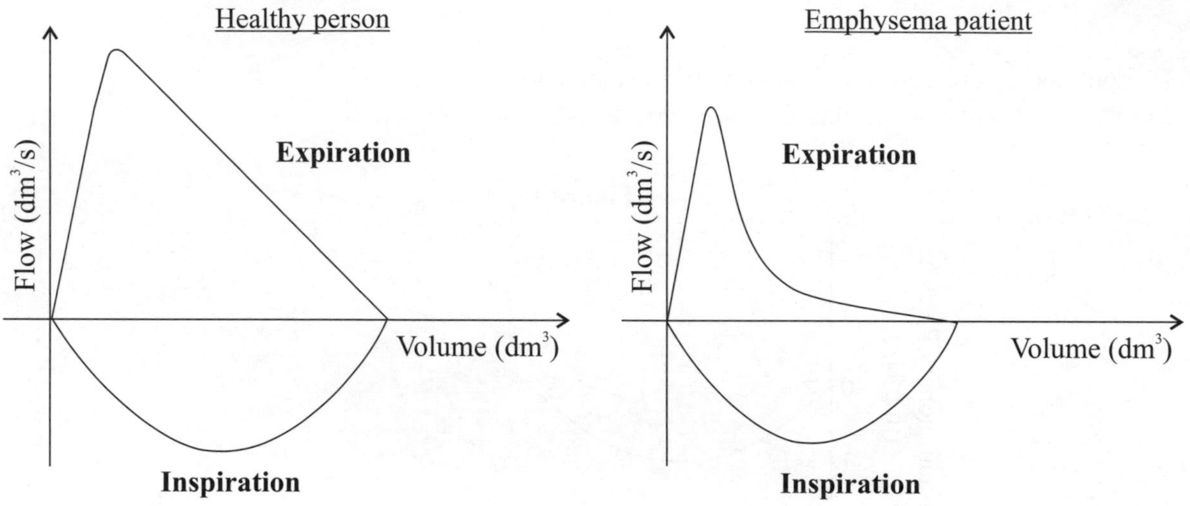

3.2 Suggest why the inspiration section of the emphysema patient's flow-volume loop is similar to that of the healthy person's, but the expiration section of the loop is not.

..............................................................................................................................

..............................................................................................................................

..............................................................................................................................

..............................................................................................................................

..............................................................................................................................

**(3 marks)**

3.3 The pulmonary ventilation rate (PVR) is the volume of air inspired or expired in one minute.
A patient has a PVR of 7.60 $dm^3$ $minute^{-1}$ and takes 16 breaths per minute.
Calculate the volume of air in each breath in $cm^3$.

.......................................... $cm^3$

**(2 marks)**

4 Asbestos is a fibrous material that was commonly used in construction work in Britain until it was banned in 1999. Long-term exposure to asbestos fibres can lead to a lung condition called asbestosis.

Asbestosis involves the build up of inelastic scar tissue in the lungs.

4.1 Suggest why people with asbestosis may have a faster ventilation rate than normal.

.....................................................................................................................................

.....................................................................................................................................

.....................................................................................................................................

**(2 marks)**

**Figure 3** shows the number of death certificates per year in Great Britain, which identified asbestosis as the underlying cause, from 1978 to 2014.

**Figure 3**

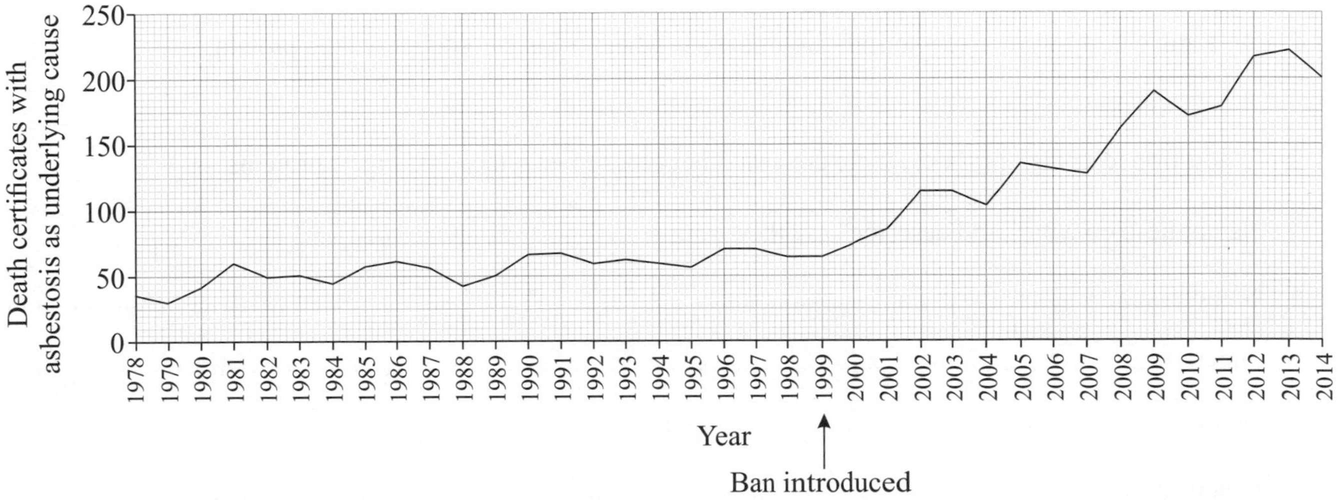

Death certificates with asbestosis as underlying cause

Year

Ban introduced

4.2 A student concludes from **Figure 3** that the asbestos ban has been unsuccessful at protecting people against asbestosis. Evaluate this conclusion.

.....................................................................................................................................

.....................................................................................................................................

.....................................................................................................................................

.....................................................................................................................................

.....................................................................................................................................

.....................................................................................................................................

.....................................................................................................................................

.....................................................................................................................................

**(4 marks)**

EXAM TIP

If you're asked to evaluate something, you need to make a judgement based on the evidence you've been given. Make sure you consider both sides of the argument in your answer — think about all the possible factors that might have affected the data you're looking at.

Score

21

# More Exchange and Transport Systems — 1

That's right — you're not done with exchange and transport systems just yet. Here's another great big section full of questions about them. You can't exchange them for something nicer, I'm afraid — get cracking.

1 Trypsin is an endopeptidase. It breaks down proteins into smaller peptides.

**Figure 1** shows a protein.

**Figure 1**

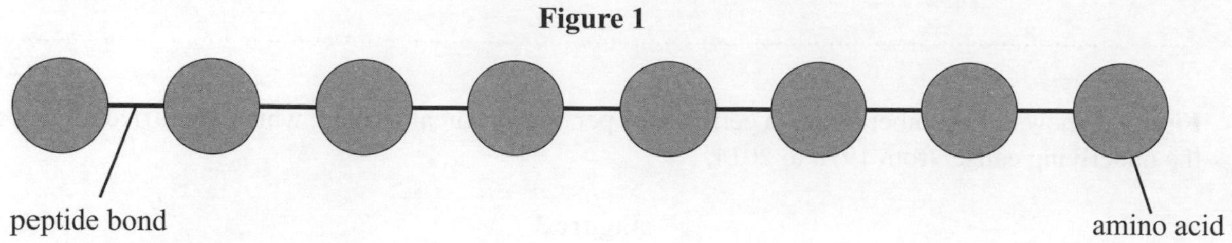


1.1 On **Figure 1**, draw an arrow to indicate **one** place where trypsin could cleave the protein.

**(1 mark)**

1.2 In addition to endopeptidases, there are **two** other types of enzymes that digest proteins.

Name these enzymes and describe how they work.

Name:.......................................................................................................

Function:.......................................................................................................

Name:.......................................................................................................

Function:.......................................................................................................

**(4 marks)**

1.3 The amino acids released by protein digestion are absorbed by the ileum epithelial cells. Explain how these amino acids are absorbed.

.......................................................................................................

.......................................................................................................

.......................................................................................................

.......................................................................................................

.......................................................................................................

.......................................................................................................

.......................................................................................................

.......................................................................................................

.......................................................................................................

.......................................................................................................

**(5 marks)**

1.4 Enteropeptidase is an enzyme produced by the cells lining the small intestine when food is ingested. The role of enteropeptidase is to convert trypsinogen, an inactive enzyme, into trypsin, its active form. A mutation in one of the genes needed to make enteropeptidase can cause enteropeptidase deficiency, which can be life-threatening.

Explain why enteropeptidase deficiency could be life-threatening.

.............................................................................................................................................

.............................................................................................................................................

.............................................................................................................................................

.............................................................................................................................................

.............................................................................................................................................

.............................................................................................................................................

**(3 marks)**

**2** Scientists investigated the breakdown of different types of commonly used oils by Lipase A in the small intestine. The results can be seen in **Figure 2**.

**Figure 2**

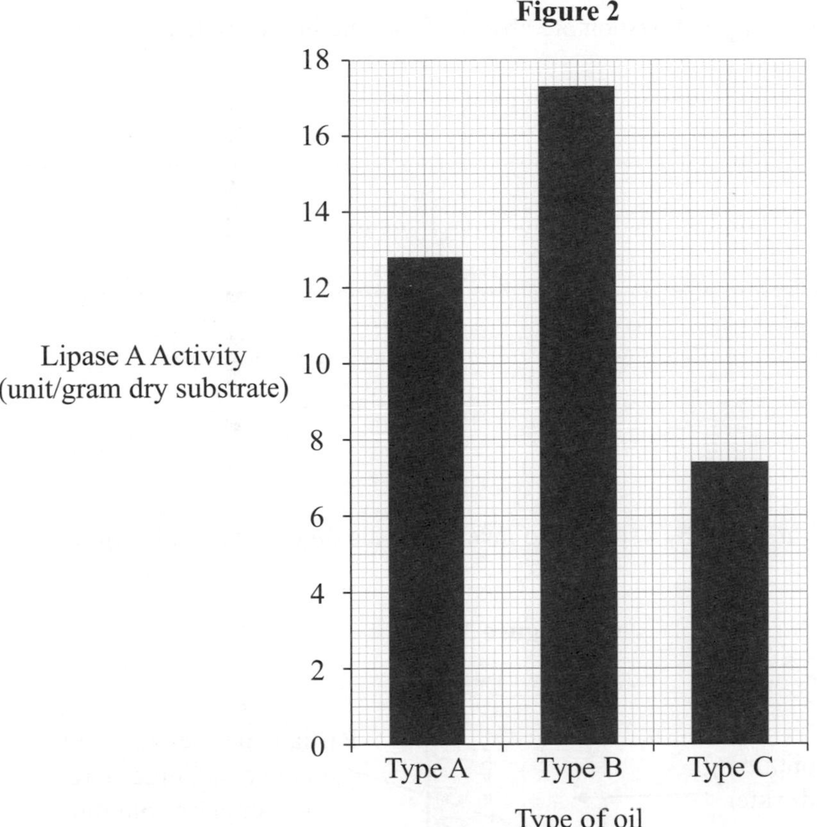


2.1 Lipase A is more effective at hydrolysing oil Type B than oil types A or C. Suggest an explanation for this.

.............................................................................................................................................

.............................................................................................................................................

.............................................................................................................................................

**(2 marks)**

2.2 Calculate the ratio of Lipase A activity for oils Type B : Type C, shown in **Figure 2**.

Ratio: ...................................... : 1

**(1 mark)**

2.3 Name **one** substance other than lipase that aids lipid digestion.

.......................................................................................................................................

**(1 mark)**

2.4 Give **two** substances that lipids are hydrolysed into.

1. .......................................................................................................................................

2. .......................................................................................................................................

**(2 marks)**

2.5 Describe how the products of lipid digestion are absorbed into the ileum epithelial cells.

.......................................................................................................................................

.......................................................................................................................................

.......................................................................................................................................

.......................................................................................................................................

.......................................................................................................................................

**(3 marks)**

**3** **Figure 3** shows a model gut set up by a student to investigate the digestion and absorption of starch.

**Figure 3**

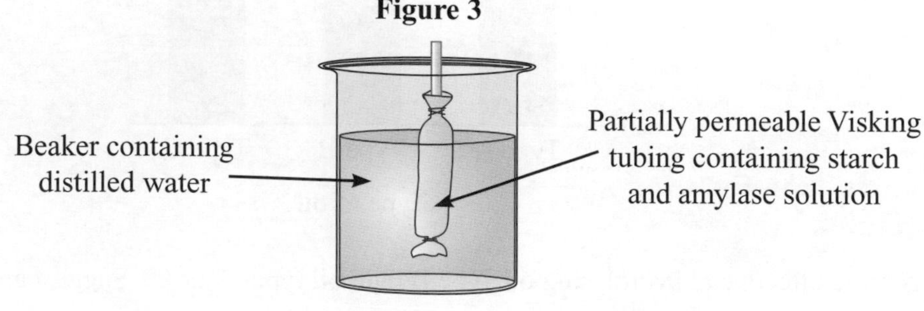


3.1 Describe how the student would set up a control for this investigation.

.......................................................................................................................................

.......................................................................................................................................

**(1 mark)**

3.2 Suggest **two** reasons why this model is not wholly representative of absorption in the gut.

1. ..............................................................................................................

..............................................................................................................

2. ..............................................................................................................

..............................................................................................................

**(2 marks)**



The contents of the Visking tubing and the beaker were tested with iodine and Benedict's reagent at the start of the experiment, and after they had been left for 20 minutes. **Table 1** shows the results of these tests.

**Table 1**

| | Iodine test result | Benedict's test result |
|---|---|---|
| Visking tubing contents at start | Positive | Negative |
| Beaker contents at start | Negative | Negative |
| Visking tubing contents after 20 minutes | Negative | Positive |
| Beaker contents after 20 minutes | Negative | Positive |

3.3 Explain the iodine test results.

..............................................................................................................

..............................................................................................................

..............................................................................................................

..............................................................................................................

..............................................................................................................

..............................................................................................................

**(4 marks)**

3.4 Explain the Benedict's test results.

..............................................................................................................

..............................................................................................................

..............................................................................................................

..............................................................................................................

..............................................................................................................

..............................................................................................................

**(4 marks)**

EXAM TIP

Often maths questions look more complicated than they actually are, because they're written in a certain context. Try not to get put off by all the words — if it's just worth one mark, the actual calculation you have to do is probably quite straightforward. Check your answer by thinking about what sort of size you'd expect the answer to be in the context of the question.

Score

33

# More Exchange and Transport Systems — 2

1 **Figure 1** shows the oxygen dissociation curves for humans and llamas, a mammal that lives at high altitudes.

**Figure 1**

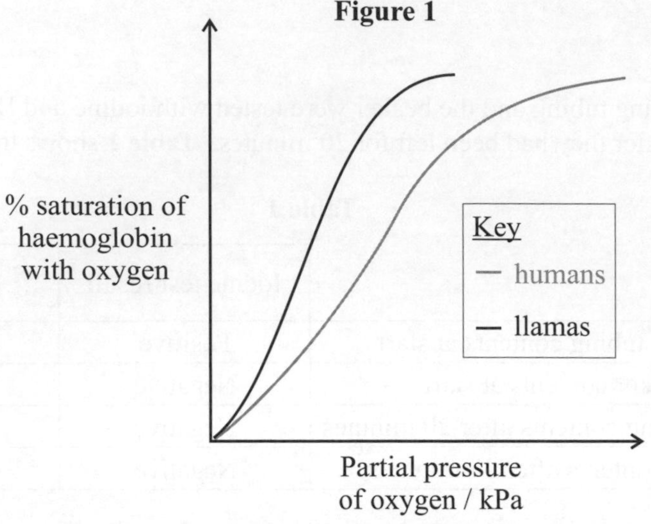


1.1 Describe and explain the shape of the oxygen dissociation curve for humans.

..........................................................................................................................................

..........................................................................................................................................

..........................................................................................................................................

..........................................................................................................................................

..........................................................................................................................................

..........................................................................................................................................

..........................................................................................................................................

..........................................................................................................................................

..........................................................................................................................................

**(5 marks)**

1.2 Explain the differences between the oxygen dissociation curves for llamas and humans.

..........................................................................................................................................

..........................................................................................................................................

..........................................................................................................................................

..........................................................................................................................................

..........................................................................................................................................

..........................................................................................................................................

**(3 marks)**

**Figure 2** shows the oxygen dissociation curve for a person who is exercising, alongside a person who is not exercising.

**Figure 2**

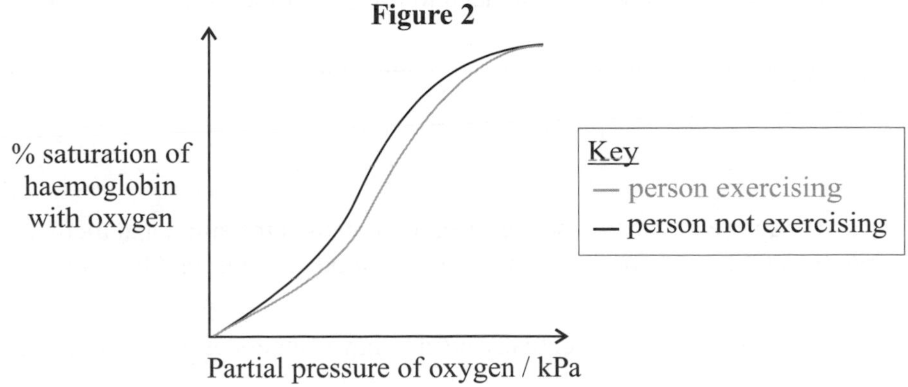


1.3 Explain why the oxygen dissociation curve for the person exercising is to the right of the oxygen dissociation curve for the person who is not exercising.

.....................................................................................................................................

.....................................................................................................................................

.....................................................................................................................................

**(3 marks)**

2 **Figure 3** shows a diagram of a mammalian heart.

**Figure 3**

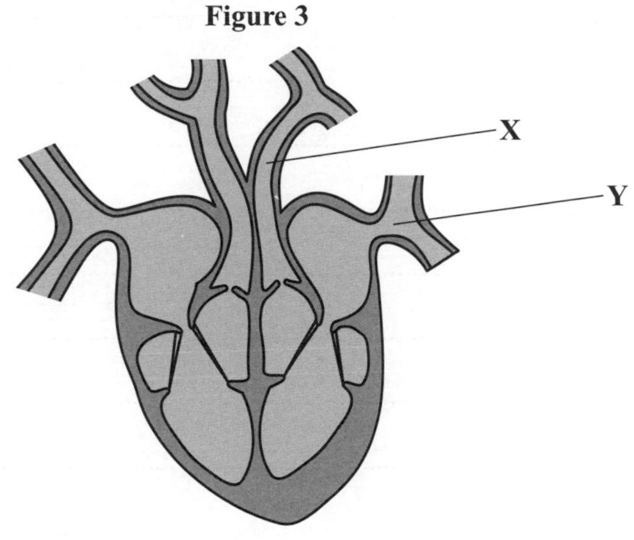


2.1 Name the parts of the heart labelled **X** and **Y**.

Name of **X** .....................................................................................................................

Name of **Y** .....................................................................................................................

**(2 marks)**

A student carried out a dissection of a mammalian heart.

2.2 State **three** precautions that must be taken in order to safely carry out a dissection.

1. .....................................................................................................................

2. .....................................................................................................................

3. .....................................................................................................................

**(3 marks)**

The student produced a biological drawing of the heart.

2.3 Give **one** instruction that the student would need to follow in order to produce a clear and useful drawing.

..........................................................................................................................................

**(1 mark)**

**3** Buerger's disease is a type of cardiovascular disease. It causes the small and medium arteries and veins in the hands and feet to experience thrombosis (blood clotting) and become inflamed.

3.1 People with Buerger's disease may eventually need to have fingers or toes amputated. Suggest why.

..........................................................................................................................................

..........................................................................................................................................

..........................................................................................................................................

..........................................................................................................................................

**(2 marks)**

Buerger's disease causes a reduction in the volume of tissue fluid that passes through capillary beds.

3.2 Describe how tissue fluid is formed in healthy tissues, and how it is returned to the circulatory system.

..........................................................................................................................................

..........................................................................................................................................

..........................................................................................................................................

..........................................................................................................................................

..........................................................................................................................................

..........................................................................................................................................

..........................................................................................................................................

..........................................................................................................................................

**(5 marks)**

Capillary beds are important exchange surfaces.

3.3 Explain **one** way in which the structure of capillaries helps them carry out their function.

..........................................................................................................................................

..........................................................................................................................................

**(1 mark)**

EXAM TIP

Don't forget that you should also revise the practicals you did in class — the exam will test you on your practical skills as well as the theory. By the time you're sitting the exam, it might have been a while since you did some of the practicals, so make sure you've reminded yourself of what you did, the equipment you used, and the safety precautions you had to take.

Score

25

# More Exchange and Transport Systems — 3

1 **Figure 1** shows a cross-section of the human heart.

**Figure 1**

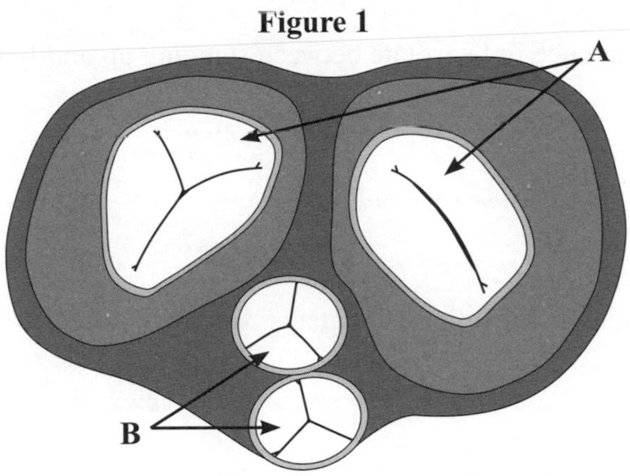


1.1 What is the role of the valves labelled **A** in **Figure 1**?

.............................................................................................................................................

.............................................................................................................................................

.............................................................................................................................................

**(2 marks)**

1.2 In terms of pressure changes in the heart, explain what causes the valves labelled **B** in **Figure 1** to open.

.............................................................................................................................................

.............................................................................................................................................

**(1 mark)**

Cardiac output is the volume of blood pumped out of the left ventricle in one minute.
Scientists investigated the effect of body position on heart rate and cardiac output.
**Table 1** shows their results.

**Table 1**

| | Standing up | Lying down |
|---|---|---|
| Mean heart rate / bpm | 74 | 57 |
| Mean cardiac output / $cm^3$ $min^{-1}$ | 4700 | 4700 |
| Mean stroke volume / $cm^3$ | | |

1.3 The stroke volume is the volume of blood that is pumped out by the left ventricle in one cardiac cycle.
Use the information in **Table 1** to complete the table to show the mean stroke volume.

**(1 mark)**

Use the information you've been given in the question to come up with a formula linking stroke volume, cardiac output and heart rate. Then substitute in the numbers from the table.

1.4 The scientists ensured that the participants of the investigation had been in the required position for five minutes before they recorded these measurements. Suggest why.

..........................................................................................................................................

..........................................................................................................................................

**(1 mark)**

1.5 Suggest why there is a difference in heart rate between standing up and lying down in **Table 1**.

..........................................................................................................................................

..........................................................................................................................................

**(1 mark)**

1.6 Explain why the scientists used 'mean' measurements.

..........................................................................................................................................

..........................................................................................................................................

**(1 mark)**

**2** **Figure 2** shows the pressure changes in an individual's heart during the cardiac cycle.

**Figure 2**

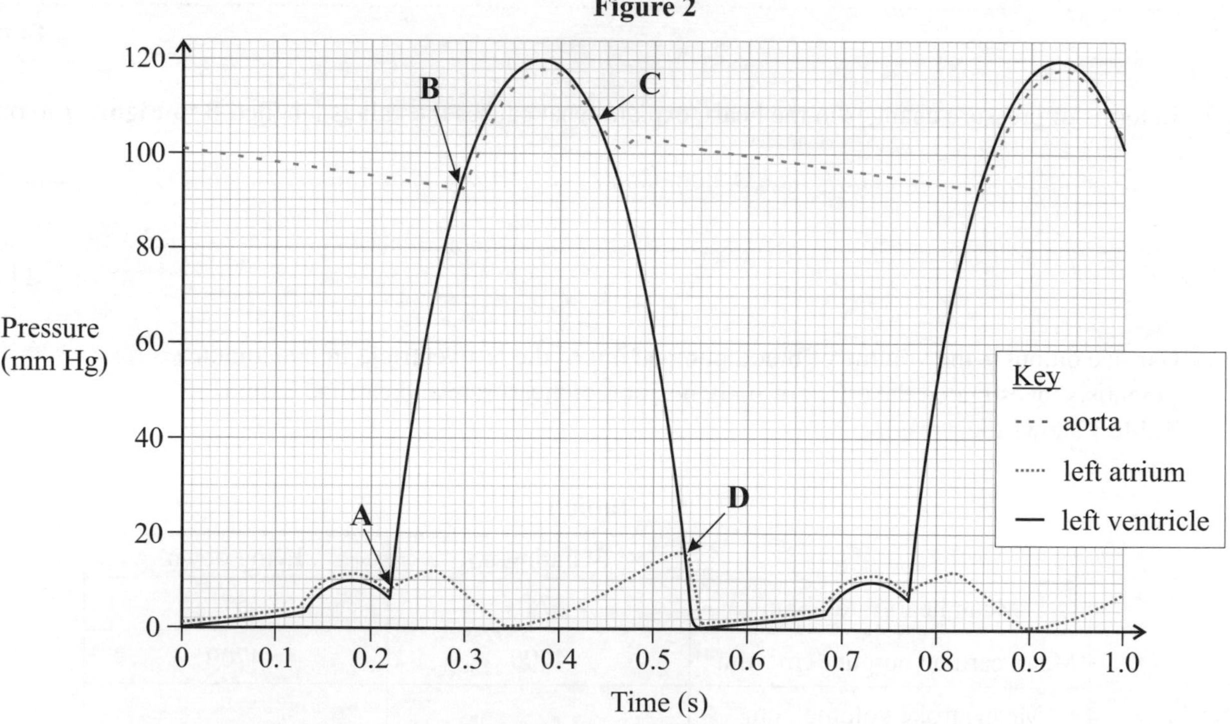


2.1 Calculate the heart rate for the individual shown in **Figure 2**.

.................. beats per minute

**(1 mark)**

2.2 When on **Figure 2** does the left atrium start to contract?

Hint: when a chamber contracts, there's a sudden rise in pressure inside the chamber.

................................ seconds
**(1 mark)**

2.3 Describe and explain the events that are occurring at points **A** to **D** on **Figure 2**.

.......................................................................................................................................

.......................................................................................................................................

.......................................................................................................................................

.......................................................................................................................................

.......................................................................................................................................

.......................................................................................................................................

.......................................................................................................................................

.......................................................................................................................................

.......................................................................................................................................

.......................................................................................................................................

.......................................................................................................................................

.......................................................................................................................................

.......................................................................................................................................

**(6 marks)**

2.4 Explain the difference between the maximum pressures of the left atrium and the left ventricle of the heart.

.......................................................................................................................................

.......................................................................................................................................

.......................................................................................................................................

**(1 mark)**

2.5 Using your own knowledge and information from **Figure 2**, explain **one** way in which the aorta is adapted for its function.

.......................................................................................................................................

.......................................................................................................................................

.......................................................................................................................................

**(2 marks)**

EXAM TIP

When you're writing a long answer, you should think about how many marks it's worth, and make sure you've written enough separate things that would each get a mark. Don't just fill up the lines with empty waffle and assume you've written enough — you need to include specific biological terms and write in sufficient detail to get every mark available.

Score

18

# More Exchange and Transport Systems — 4

**1** A student used a potometer to investigate transpiration in a plant. **Figure 1** shows how the potometer was set up. The student closed the tap, then took the capillary tube out of the beaker of water long enough for an air bubble to form. She then recorded the amount of time it took for the air bubble to move between the two markers, and used it to calculate the transpiration rate.

**Figure 1**

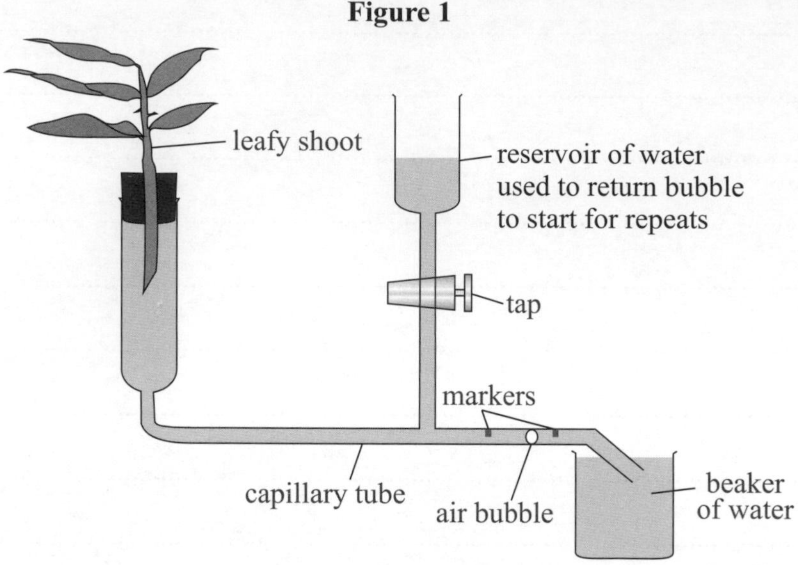


1.1 When setting up this experiment, it is important that water does not touch the leaves. Using your knowledge of water transport in plants, explain why.

..........

..........

..........

**(2 marks)**

The student used the potometer to investigate the effect of temperature on the transpiration rate. The results are shown in **Table 1**.

**Table 1**

| Temperature / °C | Mean transpiration rate / $cm^3$ per minute |
|---|---|
| 20 | 0.20 |
| 30 | 0.34 |
| 40 | 0.85 |
| 50 | 1.24 |
| 60 | 1.36 |

1.2 Describe and explain the relationship between the temperature and the transpiration rate in **Table 1**.

..........

..........

..........

..........

..........

**(3 marks)**

**2** Xylem vessels are found running from the roots to the leaves in plants. Scientists measured the rate of water flow through the xylem of a plant in its natural environment at different times of the day. The results are presented in **Table 2**.

**Table 2**

| Time of day | Rate of water flow in xylem / $mm^3$ $second^{-1}$ |
|---|---|
| 00:00 | 0.8 |
| 06:00 | 2.8 |
| 12:00 | 4.5 |
| 18:00 | 3.0 |

2.1 Using your knowledge of water transport in the xylem, explain the difference in the results between 00:00 and 12:00 in **Table 2**.

.......................................................................................................................................................

.......................................................................................................................................................

.......................................................................................................................................................

.......................................................................................................................................................

**(3 marks)**

In order to investigate the structure of the xylem, the scientists also carried out a dissection on a leaf of the plant.

2.2 Suggest why the scientists kept the dissected plant tissue in water until they were ready to view the cells.

.......................................................................................................................................................

.......................................................................................................................................................

**(1 mark)**

2.3 Suggest a step in the dissection that the scientists would have carried out in order to observe the xylem vessels under a microscope.

.......................................................................................................................................................

.......................................................................................................................................................

**(1 mark)**

**3** Translocation in a plant describes the movement of solutes to where they are needed within the plant.

3.1 When treated with metabolic inhibitors, translocation in a plant stops. Explain why.

.......................................................................................................................................................

.......................................................................................................................................................

.......................................................................................................................................................

**(2 marks)**

**Figure 2** represents the flow of solutes in the phloem of a tree, according to the mass flow hypothesis.

**Figure 2**

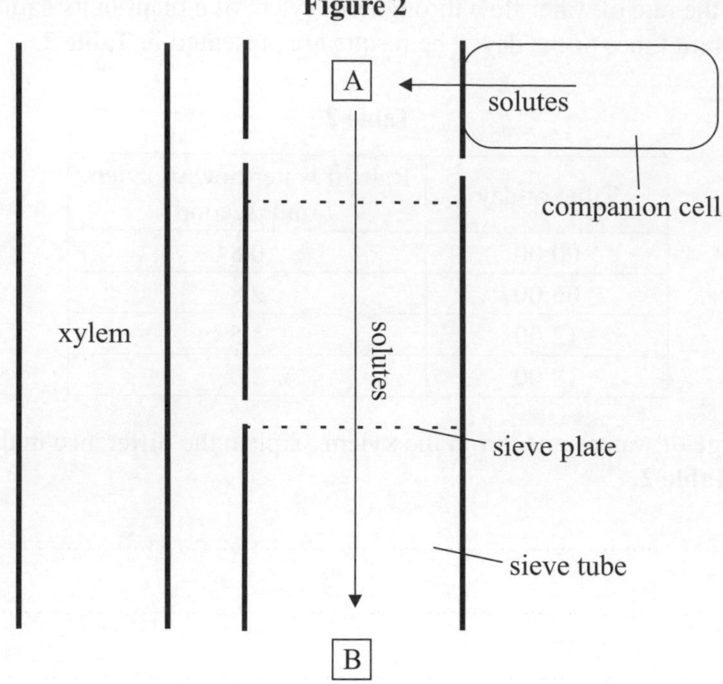


3.2 Describe and explain how the level of pressure at point **A** in **Figure 2** differs to that at point **B**.

........................................................................................................................................

........................................................................................................................................

........................................................................................................................................

........................................................................................................................................

**(3 marks)**

A ring of bark is removed from the tree at point **B**.

3.3 Explain how this would affect the concentration of solutes at point **A**, according to the mass flow hypothesis.

........................................................................................................................................

........................................................................................................................................

**(2 marks)**

3.4 Other than a ringing experiment, describe **one** other type of experiment that could be carried out to monitor translocation in trees.

........................................................................................................................................

........................................................................................................................................

........................................................................................................................................

........................................................................................................................................

**(3 marks)**

If a question asks you to 'describe and explain' something, make sure you do both. 'Describing' means giving an account of something, e.g. saying how a variable changes in a table or graph, whereas 'explaining' means setting out reasons, e.g. saying why the variable changes. Doing just one or the other will mean you miss out on marks.

Score

20

# DNA, RNA and Protein Synthesis

Protein synthesis isn't easy, but imagine the warm, glowing feeling you'll get once you've worked your way through all these questions on it. Can't imagine it? Never mind, give the questions a go and you'll soon feel it.

**1** The average human cell contains around 2 m of DNA.
The average human cell nucleus is only 10 μm in diameter.

1.1 Describe how the DNA in a eukaryotic cell is arranged so that it can fit into the nucleus.

..........................................................................................................................................

..........................................................................................................................................

**(2 marks)**

1.2 Prokaryotic DNA is not stored in a nucleus.
Give **one** other difference between the way that DNA is arranged in eukaryotic cells and prokaryotic cells.

..........................................................................................................................................

..........................................................................................................................................

**(1 mark)**

It is estimated that the DNA in a human cell contains around 20 000 protein-encoding genes.
These genes correspond to only 1.5% of the DNA sequence.

1.3 Using the information provided above, calculate the average length of a human gene in metres.

Length of gene = ........................................... m

**(2 marks)**

1.4 What name is given to the complete set of genes present in a cell?

..........................................................................................................................................

**(1 mark)**

1.5 What name is given to the complete set of proteins that a cell is able to produce?

..........................................................................................................................................

**(1 mark)**

In prokaryotes, around 90% of the DNA is protein-encoding.

1.6 Suggest **two** reasons why prokaryotes have a much greater percentage of protein-encoding DNA than humans.

1. ......................................................................................................................................

2. ......................................................................................................................................

**(2 marks)**

1.7 Protein-encoding DNA leads to the production of mRNA.
Other parts of the DNA encode functional RNA. Give **two** examples of functional RNA.

1. ......................................................................................................................................

2. ......................................................................................................................................

**(2 marks)**

**2** Leigh syndrome is a metabolic disorder that affects the central nervous system. It can be caused by a mutation in the MT-ATP6 gene, which is located in the mitochondrial DNA.

2.1 Give **two** differences between the structure of DNA found in the mitochondria and the structure of DNA found in the nucleus.

1. ..........................................................................................................

2. ..........................................................................................................

**(2 marks)**

2.2 What name is given to the location that a gene occupies on a particular DNA molecule?

**A** Intron ☐

**B** Exon ☐

**C** Allele ☐

**D** Locus ☐

**(1 mark)**

**Table 1** contains some of the DNA codons that code for particular amino acids.

**Table 1**

| Amino acid | DNA codon |
|---|---|
| Isoleucine | ATT, ATC, ATA |
| Glutamic acid | GAA, GAG |
| Leucine | CTG, TTA, TTG |
| Methionine | ATG |
| Valine | GTT, GTC, GTA, GTG |
| Arginine | CGG, AGA |
| Alanine | GCT, GCC, GCA, GCG |

2.3 Give **one** piece of evidence from **Table 1** that shows the genetic code is degenerate.

..........................................................................................................

..........................................................................................................

**(1 mark)**

**Figure 1** shows **one** of the mutations in the MT-ATP6 gene that can cause Leigh syndrome.

**Figure 1**

**Original gene:** CAA CCA ATA GCC C**T**G GCC GTA

**Mutated gene:** CAA CCA ATA GCC C**G**G GCC GTA

**Codon position:** 152 153 154 155 156 157 158

2.4 Describe the effect that the mutation shown in **Figure 1** will have on the mRNA sequence produced from the MT-ATP6 gene.

..........................................................................................................

..........................................................................................................

**(1 mark)**

2.5 Using **Table 1** for reference, describe the effect that the mutation shown in **Figure 1** will have on the amino acid sequence produced from the MT-ATP6 gene.

.......................................................................................................................................

.......................................................................................................................................

**(1 mark)**

2.6 MT-ATP6 codes for a subunit of ATP synthase, an enzyme involved in respiration.
Explain how a change in its amino acid sequence could affect the function of ATP synthase.

.......................................................................................................................................

.......................................................................................................................................

.......................................................................................................................................

**(3 marks)**

2.7 Describe how the mRNA produced from the MT-ATP6 gene is translated into a protein.

.......................................................................................................................................

.......................................................................................................................................

.......................................................................................................................................

.......................................................................................................................................

.......................................................................................................................................

.......................................................................................................................................

.......................................................................................................................................

**(5 marks)**

**3** Transcriptomics involves studying the RNA present in a cell.
One technique involved in transcriptomics is described in **Figure 2**.

**Figure 2**

| All of the mRNA is extracted from a cell. | → | An enzyme is used to convert the mRNA into complementary DNA (cDNA). | → | The sequence of the cDNA molecules is determined. This allows the mRNA molecules to be identified. | → | The data is analysed to determine the level of mRNA expression. |
|---|---|---|---|---|---|---|

3.1 Describe how mRNA is produced from DNA by RNA polymerase.

.......................................................................................................................................

.......................................................................................................................................

.......................................................................................................................................

.......................................................................................................................................

.......................................................................................................................................

.......................................................................................................................................

**(4 marks)**

A team of scientists have developed a new drug. The team used the method in **Figure 2** to investigate how the levels of three different mRNA molecules changed when eukaryotic cells were treated with the drug.

**Figure 3** shows two images. One represents the cDNA for one of the mRNA molecules. The other represents the original DNA strand from which the mRNA was produced in the nucleus.

**Figure 3**

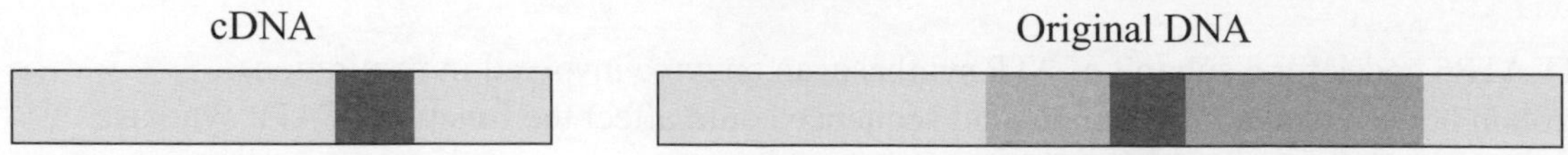

cDNA | Original DNA

3.2 Explain why the cDNA and the original DNA shown in **Figure 3** are different.

..........

..........

..........

**(2 marks)**

The results of the scientists' experiment are shown in **Figure 4**.

**Figure 4**

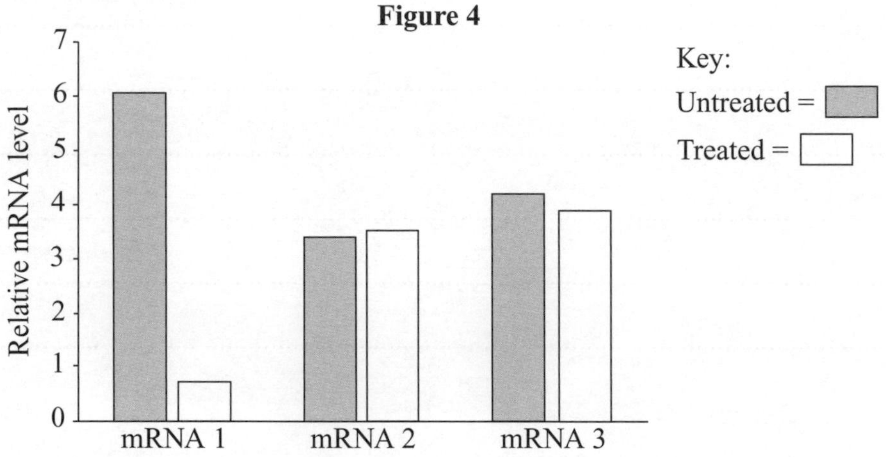

The scientists hypothesised that the new drug had two possible methods of action:
Method 1: By preventing RNA polymerase from working.
Method 2: By destroying particular mRNA sequences.

3.3 With reference to **Figure 4**, explain why the drug cannot be acting via Method 1.

..........

..........

..........

**(2 marks)**

3.4 Explain how the results shown in **Figure 4** can be explained if the drug acts via Method 2.

..........

..........

..........

**(2 marks)**

EXAM TIP

Make sure you know the basics of DNA and RNA structure, as well as the relationship between the base sequence in DNA, mRNA and tRNA. If you do, questions like 2.4 will be easy marks in the exam. It's important to remember that U replaces T in RNA too.

Score

35

# Diversity, Classification and Variation — 1

It is due to variations in the genetic code that there is such a great diversity of life on Earth. And because there's so much diversity, scientists find it easier to classify organisms into groups. There's a lot to remember for this section, but don't worry — these questions are here to help you make sure you're all set for your exams.

1 **Figure 1** is a phylogenetic tree. It shows how different species from the order Carnivora are related.

**Figure 1**

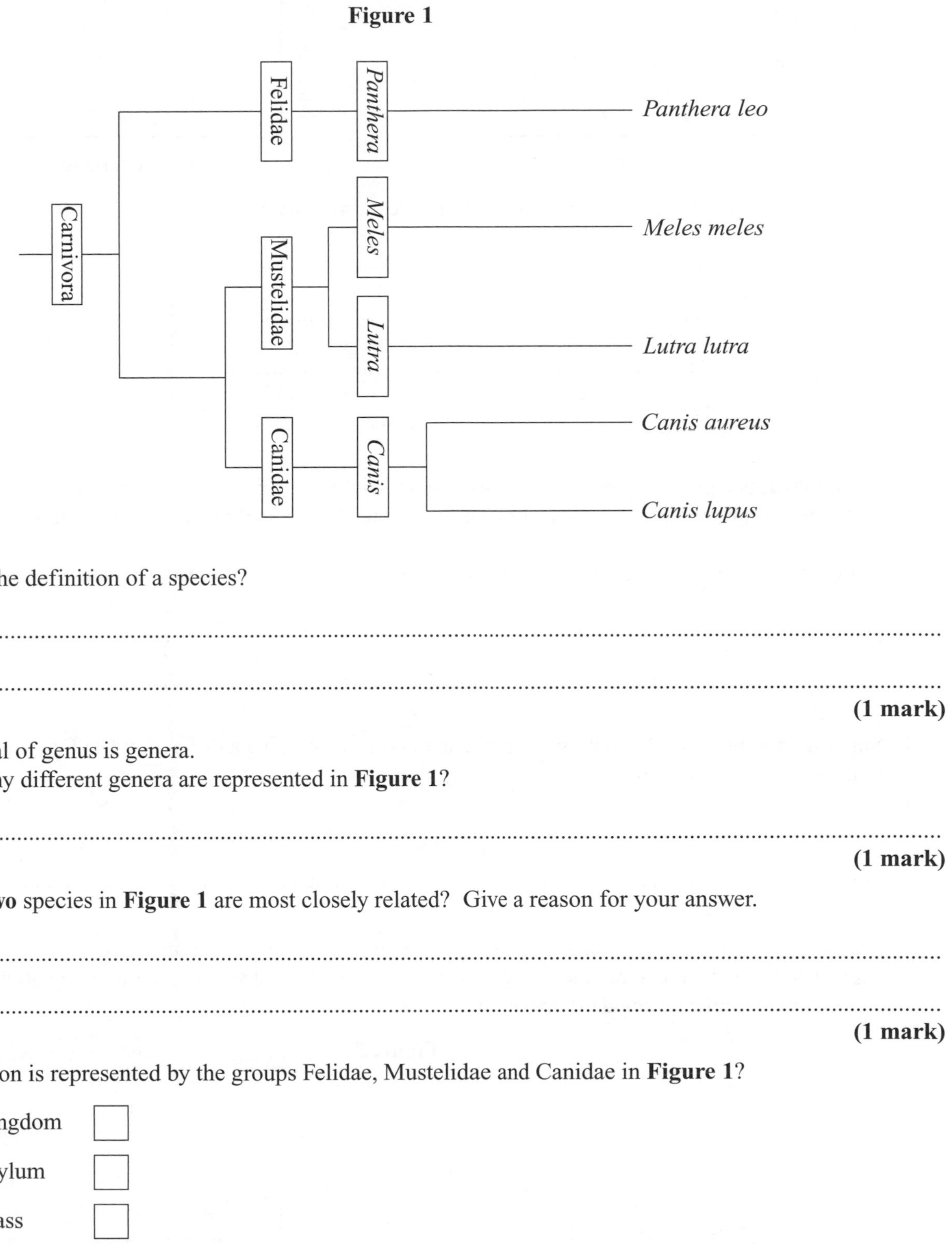


1.1 What is the definition of a species?

........................................................................................................................................

........................................................................................................................................

**(1 mark)**

1.2 The plural of genus is genera.
How many different genera are represented in **Figure 1**?

........................................................................................................................................

**(1 mark)**

1.3 Which **two** species in **Figure 1** are most closely related? Give a reason for your answer.

........................................................................................................................................

........................................................................................................................................

**(1 mark)**

1.4 What taxon is represented by the groups Felidae, Mustelidae and Canidae in **Figure 1**?

**A** Kingdom ☐

**B** Phylum ☐

**C** Class ☐

**D** Family ☐

**(1 mark)**

**2** Species become better adapted to their environment via the process of natural selection.

**Figure 2** shows two populations (**A** and **B**) experiencing natural selection.

**Figure 2**

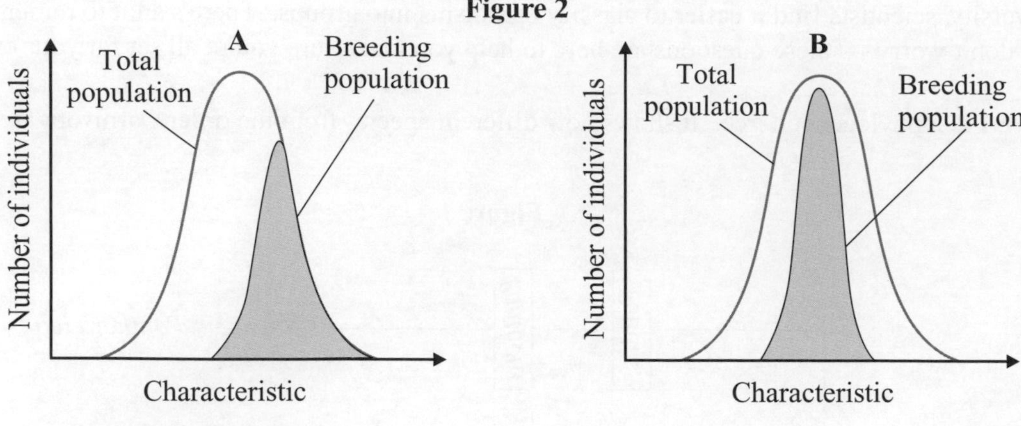


2.1 Compare and contrast the **two** types of natural selection shown in **Figure 2**.

..........................................................................................................................................

..........................................................................................................................................

..........................................................................................................................................

..........................................................................................................................................

**(3 marks)**

In **Figure 2**, one graph represents the selection on height faced by a plant population in a dense forest. The other graph represents the selection on height faced by a plant population in open grassland.

2.2 Using this information, state which population (**A** or **B**) is from the forest. Explain your answer.

..........................................................................................................................................

..........................................................................................................................................

**(2 marks)**

2.3 Suggest why the plant population in open grassland is undergoing a different type of selection to the one in the dense forest.

..........................................................................................................................................

..........................................................................................................................................

**(1 mark)**

Clutch size is the number of eggs laid by a female bird during one breeding season.
**Figure 3** shows the mean number of eggs in a clutch over several years for a bird population.
The error bars indicate standard deviation.

**Figure 3**

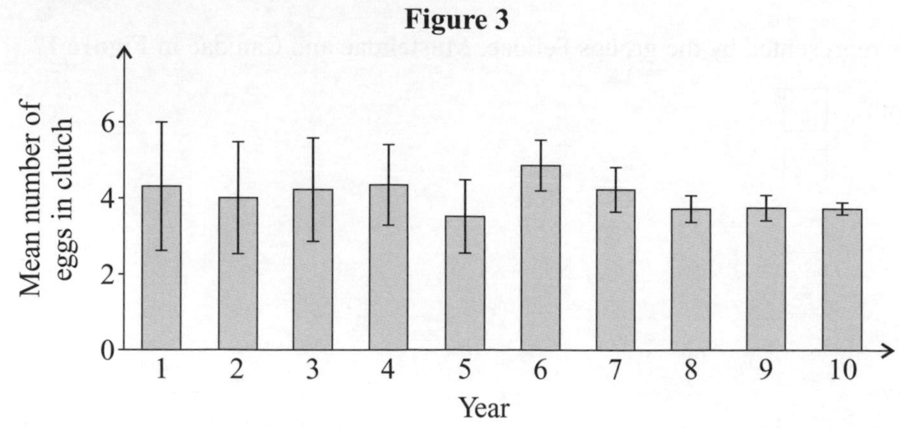

2.4 Suggest an explanation for the changes shown in **Figure 3**.

..........

..........

..........

..........

**(3 marks)**

**3** When classifying organisms, scientists often look at the proteins found within the organisms.

3.1 Explain why proteins can be analysed to help classify organisms.

..........

..........

..........

**(3 marks)**

Scientists compared the amino acid sequence of a protein in four species, to that in humans. They counted the differences in each amino acid sequence, compared to the sequence in humans. The data obtained is presented in **Table 1**.

**Table 1**

| Species | Number of differences in amino acid sequence compared to human protein |
|---|---|
| A | 25 |
| B | 7 |
| C | 1 |
| D | 7 |

3.2 Using the information in **Table 1**, discuss the scientists' results.

..........

..........

..........

**(2 marks)**

3.3 It was concluded that species **B** and **D** were more closely related to each other than they were to humans. Explain why this is not a valid conclusion for this data.

..........

..........

**(1 mark)**

EXAM TIP

Standard deviation is a measure of the variation around the mean. Error bars can be used to show standard deviation in graphs. Put simply — the shorter the bar, the smaller the standard deviation and the less spread out the data is. Not all error bars represent standard deviation though, so make sure you read the question carefully to figure out what they mean.

Score

19

# Diversity, Classification and Variation — 2

**1** Scientists investigated the diversity of plants in an ungrazed field. The data obtained is shown in **Table 1**.

**Table 1**

| Species | Number of individual plants counted in different quadrats | | | | | Mean number counted |
|---|---|---|---|---|---|---|
| Rapeseed | 24 | 46 | 32 | 28 | 32 | |
| Common sunflower | 1 | 0 | 2 | 1 | 1 | |
| Common poppy | 8 | 12 | 6 | 10 | 8 | |
| Creeping thistle | 13 | 14 | 7 | 15 | 13 | |

1.1 Complete **Table 1** to show the mean number of each species counted.

**(1 mark)**

1.2 Using the mean values you added to **Table 1** and the formula provided below, calculate the index of diversity for plants in this field. Show your working.

$$d = \frac{N(N-1)}{\Sigma n(n-1)}$$

where $N$ = total number of organisms of all species
and $n$ = total number of organisms of one species

$d$ = ..........................................

**(2 marks)**

The scientists then gathered data in a second field on which farm animals were allowed to graze. The mean number of creeping thistle was much lower in the second field than in the first.

1.3 The scientists wanted to determine if the difference in means between the two fields was significant. State which statistical test they could have used to determine this. Explain your choice.

....................................................................................................

....................................................................................................

**(2 marks)**

1.4 Further investigations in both fields showed the overall biodiversity of the grazed field to be lower than that of the ungrazed field. Suggest an explanation for this.

....................................................................................................

....................................................................................................

....................................................................................................

**(2 marks)**

**2** Scientists wanted to investigate the impact of different farming practices on ladybird biodiversity. To do so, they counted the number of different ladybird species on organic and conventional farms. This allowed them to compare the species richness of the ladybirds in the different types of farm.

2.1 Explain why it may have been more useful for the scientists to compare indexes of diversity for their investigation.

..........................................................................................................................

..........................................................................................................................

..........................................................................................................................

**(2 marks)**

The scientists' data can be seen in **Figure 1**. The error bars indicate standard deviation.

**Figure 1**

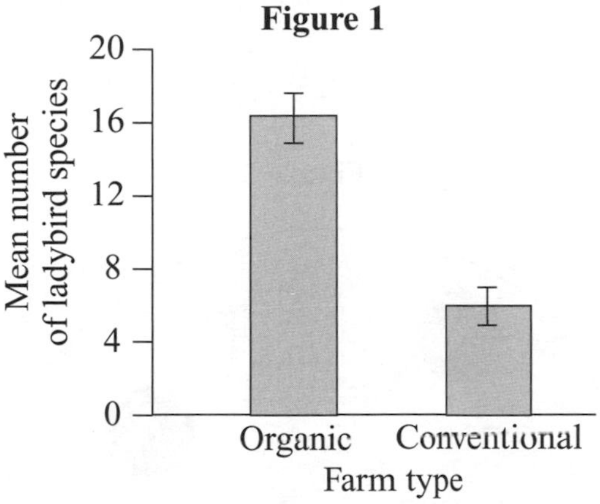

2.2 The scientists concluded that conventional farming had a much greater impact on the number of ladybird species than organic farming. Use the data in **Figure 1** to evaluate this claim.

..........................................................................................................................

..........................................................................................................................

..........................................................................................................................

..........................................................................................................................

..........................................................................................................................

**(3 marks)**

2.3 Describe and explain **two** ways in which the scientists could have ensured that the results they obtained were representative of the farms sampled.

1. ......................................................................................................................

2. ......................................................................................................................

**(2 marks)**

**3** A student wanted to investigate the effectiveness of different types of antibacterial hand sanitiser against a type of bacteria found on the surface of the skin. She was provided with paper discs, three different types of hand sanitiser, a bottle of bacterial broth culture and an agar plate.

3.1 The agar plate that the student used would have first been autoclaved. Explain why.

..........................................................................................................................

..........................................................................................................................

**(2 marks)**

3.2 Describe a method that the student could use for her investigation.
Include details of the aseptic techniques she should carry out.

**(5 marks)**

**Figure 2** shows the student's results.

**Figure 2**

Paper discs

A

B

D

C

Agar plate

3.3 Disc **A** did not contain any antibacterial hand sanitiser. Explain why it was used.

**(2 marks)**

The area of the inhibition zone surrounding each paper disc indicates the effectiveness of the antibacterial hand sanitiser.

3.4 Complete **Table 2** by calculating the areas of the inhibition zones in **Figure 2**.

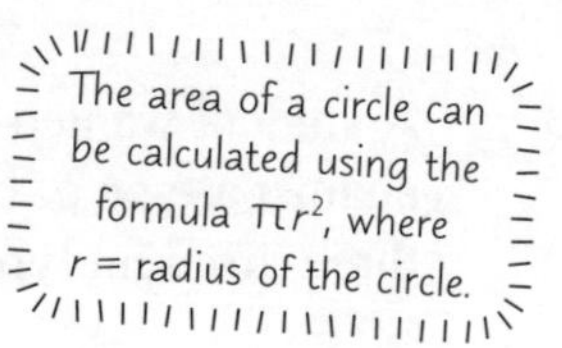

The area of a circle can be calculated using the formula πr², where r = radius of the circle.


**Table 2**

| Disc | Area of Inhibition Zone / $mm^2$ |
|---|---|
| B | |
| C | |
| D | |

**(1 mark)**

**4** Gametes are produced by meiosis. Errors occurring in meiosis can lead to significant health problems.

4.1 Explain how meiosis gives rise to genetic variation.

**(4 marks)**

4.2 The diploid number for human cells is 46. Using the formula provided below, calculate the possible number of different combinations of chromosomes following meiosis in humans.

number of combinations = $2^n$
where $n$ = the number of homologous chromosome pairs

number of different combinations of chromosomes = ..........................................

**(1 mark)**

Patau syndrome is a rare chromosomal disorder.
**Figure 3** shows the chromosomes of a male with Patau syndrome.

**Figure 3**

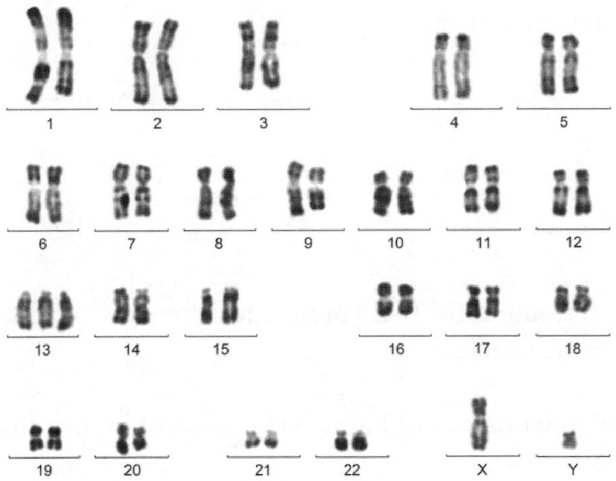

Pr Philippe VAGO, ISM/SCIENCE PHOTO LIBRARY

4.3 Using **Figure 3**, suggest and explain how events in meiosis can cause Patau syndrome.

**(4 marks)**

EXAM TIP

Phew. There's a lot of maths on these pages. The question might seem simple if you're given the formula, but it's still easy to make mistakes. You need to make sure that you're substituting the correct numbers into the formula. For example, with the index of diversity formula, make sure you don't get 'N' (number of all organisms) and 'n' (number of one species) mixed up.

Score

33

# Diversity, Classification and Variation — 3

**1** Scientists investigated whether different fish species showed any preference for slow- or fast-moving water in a river. The scientists set up a trap in an area of slow-moving water and another in an area of fast-moving water in the same river. They then counted the number of each fish species caught.

The scientists analysed the results for each species using a Student's t-test. This allowed them to determine whether any difference in the mean number of each species caught in each area of water was due to chance. **Table 1** shows their results.

**Table 1**

| Fish species | Mean number of fish | | t-test statistic > critical value at $P \leq 0.05$ |
|---|---|---|---|
| | Slow-moving water | Fast-moving water | |
| A | 22 | 7 | Yes |
| B | 21 | 44 | Yes |
| C | 32 | 22 | No |
| D | 96 | 15 | Yes |
| E | 10 | 28 | Yes |

1.1 Describe what the results of the t-test show.

.....................................................................................................

.....................................................................................................

.....................................................................................................

**(2 marks)**

The scientists wanted to determine if the fish's preferences for slow- or fast-flowing water were due to genetic differences between the species.

1.2 Suggest **two** factors that the scientists would have had to control in their investigation in order to determine this.

1. .....................................................................................................

2. .....................................................................................................

**(2 marks)**

Another team of scientists estimated the genetic diversity of one of the fish populations.

1.3 Describe and explain **one** technique they could have used to do this.

.....................................................................................................

.....................................................................................................

.....................................................................................................

**(2 marks)**

1.4 Give **one** reason why genetic diversity is important for a population.

.....................................................................................................

**(1 mark)**

**2** Ampicillin is an antibiotic used to treat bacterial infections. It acts as an irreversible competitive inhibitor of transpeptidase, an enzyme required in bacterial cell wall synthesis.

**Figure 1** shows the survival rate of **two** different strains of bacteria in the presence of increasing concentrations of ampicillin.

**Figure 1**

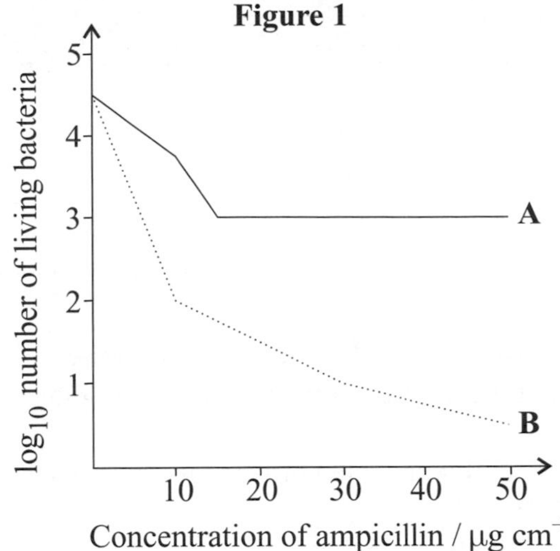


2.1 Describe **two** differences between the effect of increasing ampicillin concentration on **strain A** and the effect on **strain B**.

1. ......................................................................................................................................

......................................................................................................................................

2. ......................................................................................................................................

......................................................................................................................................

**(2 marks)**

2.2 Strain **A** was isolated from an area where high levels of ionising radiation were detected. Suggest and explain how this may have contributed to the results shown in **Figure 1**.

......................................................................................................................................

......................................................................................................................................

......................................................................................................................................

......................................................................................................................................

......................................................................................................................................

**(4 marks)**

**3** In agriculture, sheep are selectively bred for desired characteristics. This means that humans decide which sheep will breed and which will not. As a result, agricultural sheep do not always exhibit the same courtship behaviours as wild sheep.

3.1 Explain how courtship behaviour enables successful mating.

......................................................................................................................................

......................................................................................................................................

......................................................................................................................................

**(3 marks)**

Male wild bighorn sheep have large horns, which they use to fight other males for access to females.

3.2 Describe how male wild bighorn sheep may have evolved large horns through natural selection.

.............................................................................................................................

.............................................................................................................................

.............................................................................................................................

.............................................................................................................................

.............................................................................................................................

.............................................................................................................................

**(4 marks)**

Some populations of wild bighorn sheep are hunted for their horns.
There is evidence to suggest that the average horn size of male bighorn sheep is reducing in some areas.

3.3 What type of selection could be acting on male horn size in areas where hunting occurs?
Explain your answer.

.............................................................................................................................

.............................................................................................................................

.............................................................................................................................

**(3 marks)**

**Figure 2** shows the percentage mortality in populations of wild and agricultural sheep, following the outbreak of a new disease.

**Figure 2**

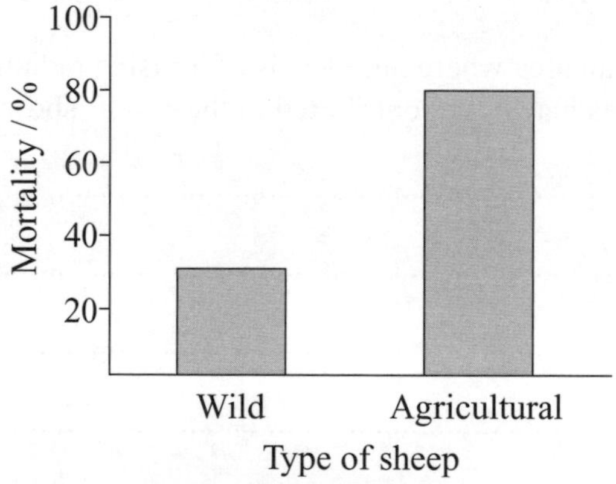

3.4 Suggest an explanation for the difference in mortality shown in **Figure 2**.

.............................................................................................................................

.............................................................................................................................

.............................................................................................................................

**(2 marks)**

EXAM TIP

If you get a question like 3.2 in the exams, you must make sure your answer relates to the specific context in the question. In other words, don't just write about how natural selection works in general — you need to relate it to the evolution of large horns in male bighorn sheep in particular. Think about how having larger horns might make the males better adapted.

Score

25

# Diversity, Classification and Variation — 4

**1** Cystic Fibrosis (CF) is a genetic condition caused by a mutation in the CFTR gene. CFTR is a channel protein present in the respiratory, digestive and reproductive tracts. It allows the movement of chloride ions across cell membranes.

Many different mutations are known to cause CF. The most common is referred to as DeltaF508. It results in the loss of an amino acid at position 508 in the CFTR protein.

1.1 State **one** way in which a mutation could result in the loss of an amino acid from a protein.

..............................................................................................................................

**(1 mark)**

One of the effects of cystic fibrosis is increased water absorption by the cells in the lungs. This means that mucus in the lungs is unusually thick and difficult to clear.

1.2 Explain how the DeltaF508 mutation could lead to increased water absorption by the cells in the lungs.

Hint: think about the function of the CFTR protein and how it might affect osmosis.

..............................................................................................................................

..............................................................................................................................

..............................................................................................................................

..............................................................................................................................

**(3 marks)**

1.3 Rarely, individuals with mutations in both of their CFTR alleles do not display all the symptoms of cystic fibrosis or their symptoms are unusually mild. Suggest an explanation for this.

..............................................................................................................................

..............................................................................................................................

**(2 marks)**

**2** Scientists are investigating the courtship behaviour of an island bird species.

**Figure 1** shows the courtship sequence of males in a single population of these birds, along with the probability that one element of the courtship behaviour leads to another element taking place.

**Figure 1**

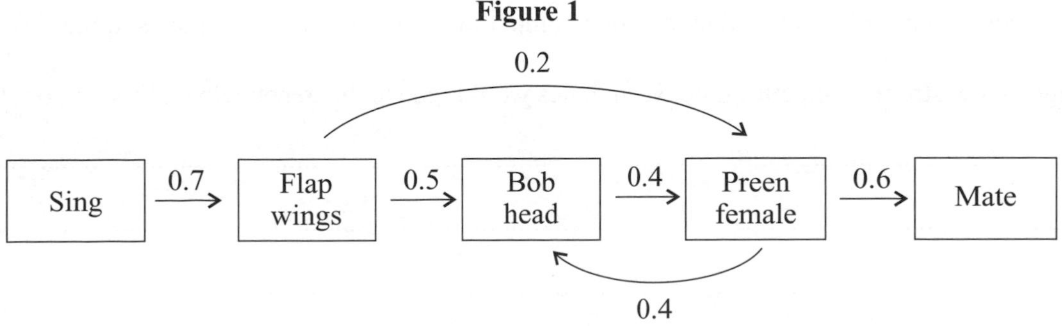


2.1 Calculate the probability that a successful mating will occur when each behaviour is carried out once.

Probability = ..............................................

**(1 mark)**

2.2 Male birds sing to attract females to them. Each bird species has a unique song. Explain why this difference in song is important.

..........................................................................................................................

..........................................................................................................................

..........................................................................................................................

**(2 marks)**

**Figure 2** shows the courtship sequence in what was thought to be another population of the same species.

**Figure 2**

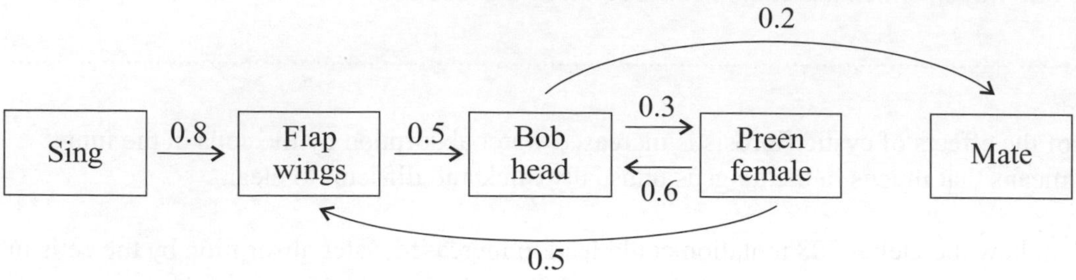

Scientists now believe that the two populations are in fact two separate species of bird.

2.3 Using the information in **Figures 1** and **2**, discuss the extent to which the two bird populations can be classified as two separate species.

..........................................................................................................................

..........................................................................................................................

..........................................................................................................................

..........................................................................................................................

..........................................................................................................................

..........................................................................................................................

**(4 marks)**

DNA evidence confirms that the two populations are separate species.

It also suggests that the population whose courtship behaviour is shown in **Figure 1** is much less genetically diverse than the population whose behaviour is shown in **Figure 2**.

Researchers think this may be due to strong competition for mates between males in the first population.

2.4 Suggest how strong competition between males would reduce the genetic diversity of a population.

..........................................................................................................................

..........................................................................................................................

..........................................................................................................................

**(2 marks)**

EXAM TIP

Remember, a mutation affects the DNA base sequence, which may alter which amino acid is coded for. A change to the amino acid sequence can alter the final structure of the protein. Imagine using rectangular bricks to build a house and then suddenly switching to round bricks.

Score

15

# Mixed Questions

Here we go: a section of juicy Mixed Questions to get your teeth into. These questions draw together different bits of biology from across the entire AS-level/Year 1 course, so they should really get those brain cells firing.

1 A student investigated the effect of pH on the activity of the enzyme lactase, which catalyses the breakdown of lactose into its monomers.

The student used the following method:

1. Add 2 ml of lactose solution and 2 ml of a pH buffer solution to a test tube. Swirl the contents of the tube gently for 10 seconds.
2. Add 2 ml of lactase solution to the test tube. Swirl the contents of the tube gently for 10 seconds.
3. After 8 minutes, dip a fresh glucose test strip into the solution in the test tube. Leave for 2 seconds and then remove.
4. After 1 minute, observe and record the colour of the test strip. Any shade of green indicates that glucose is present. If the paper remains yellow, no glucose is present.

The student repeated steps 1-4 using buffer solutions of pH 2, 4, 6, 7, 8, 10 and 12.

**Table 1** shows the results of the investigation.

**Table 1**

| pH | Glucose test result |
|---|---|
| 2 | Green |
| 4 | Green |
| 6 | Green |
| 7 | Green |
| 8 | Yellow |
| 10 | Yellow |
| 12 | Yellow |

1.1 What type of biological molecule is lactose?

**A** Nucleotide ☐

**B** Monosaccharide ☐

**C** Dipeptide ☐

**D** Disaccharide ☐

**(1 mark)**

1.2 The solution in the test tubes contains water. Explain **one** reason why water may be needed for the reaction occurring in some of the test tubes to take place.

.................................................................................................................................

.................................................................................................................................

.................................................................................................................................

**(2 marks)**

1.3 What can you conclude about the effect of pH on lactase activity from the results shown in **Table 1**? Explain your answer.

.................................................................................................................................................

.................................................................................................................................................

.................................................................................................................................................

.................................................................................................................................................

**(3 marks)**

1.4 Describe how enzyme structure is affected by pH.

.................................................................................................................................................

.................................................................................................................................................

.................................................................................................................................................

.................................................................................................................................................

**(3 marks)**

1.5 The student's method specified that all volumes and timings should have been controlled as part of her investigation. Give **two** other variables that the student should have controlled.

1. ..............................................................................................................................................

2. ..............................................................................................................................................

**(2 marks)**

1.6 Suggest how the student could continue her investigation to determine a more accurate estimate for the pH at which lactase denatures. Explain your answer.

.................................................................................................................................................

.................................................................................................................................................

.................................................................................................................................................

**(2 marks)**

1.7 Human lactase is a membrane-bound enzyme found in ileum epithelial cells.
Not all lactase is membrane-bound.
Describe **one** advantage of lactase in the human ileum being membrane-bound.

.................................................................................................................................................

.................................................................................................................................................

.................................................................................................................................................

**(1 mark)**

1.8 Most young children produce lactase, but the gene that codes for it is switched off as they get older.
In Europe, a mutation over 7000 years ago is thought to have caused this gene to remain active in adults.

Suggest why this mutation became common in Europeans.

.................................................................................................................................................

.................................................................................................................................................

.................................................................................................................................................

.................................................................................................................................................

**(3 marks)**

**2** Mitosis and meiosis are both types of cell division.

**Figure 1** represents two cells. One cell is undergoing mitosis. The other is undergoing meiosis I.

**Figure 1**

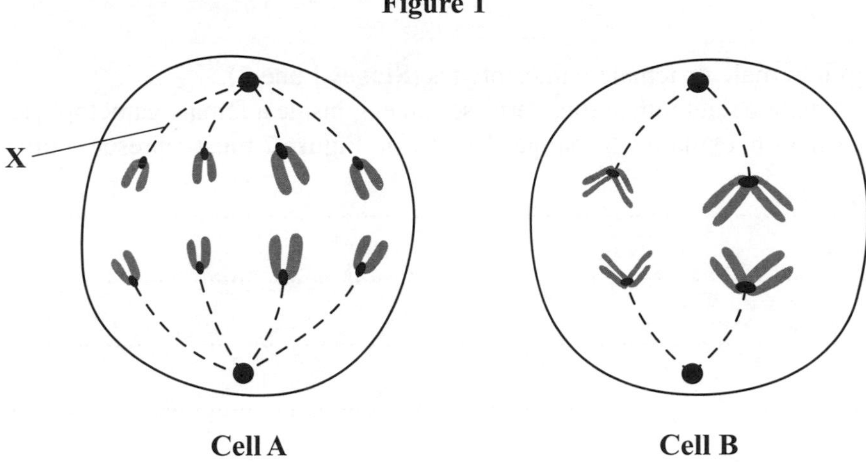


2.1 Identify the structure labelled **X**.

..........................................................................................................................................

**(1 mark)**

2.2 Which of the cells in **Figure 1** (**A** or **B**) is undergoing meiosis I?
Give a reason for your answer.

..........................................................................................................................................

..........................................................................................................................................

**(1 mark)**

**Figure 2** shows the life cycle of a type of plant called a liverwort. During the life cycle there are haploid (n) and diploid (2n) phases. Four stages of cell division are labelled.

**Figure 2**

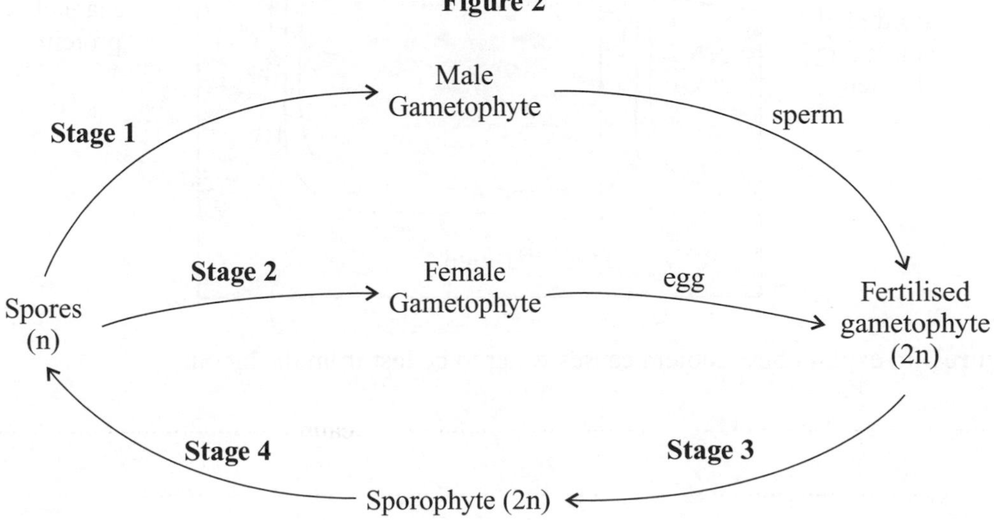


2.3 The diploid number of this liverwort is 40. How many chromosomes are present in the spore?

Number of chromosomes = ..................................

**(1 mark)**

2.4 Name the type of cell division occurring at **Stage 4** on **Figure 2**.
Give a reason for your answer.

.....................................................................................................................................

.....................................................................................................................................

**(1 mark)**

2.5 Spores develop into male or female gametophytes (**Stages 1** and **2**).
A sperm from a male gametophyte then fertilises an egg inside a female gametophyte.
Using this information, explain why **Stages 1** and **2** on **Figure 2** must represent mitosis.

.....................................................................................................................................

.....................................................................................................................................

.....................................................................................................................................

.....................................................................................................................................

**(3 marks)**

**3** *Vibrio cholerae* are pathogenic bacteria that cause the disease cholera in humans. The bacteria produce a toxin that causes $Cl^-$ channel proteins in the ileum lining to remain open. This can result in the loss of a large volume of water from the blood.

**Figure 3** shows a small section of the ileum lining.

**Figure 3**

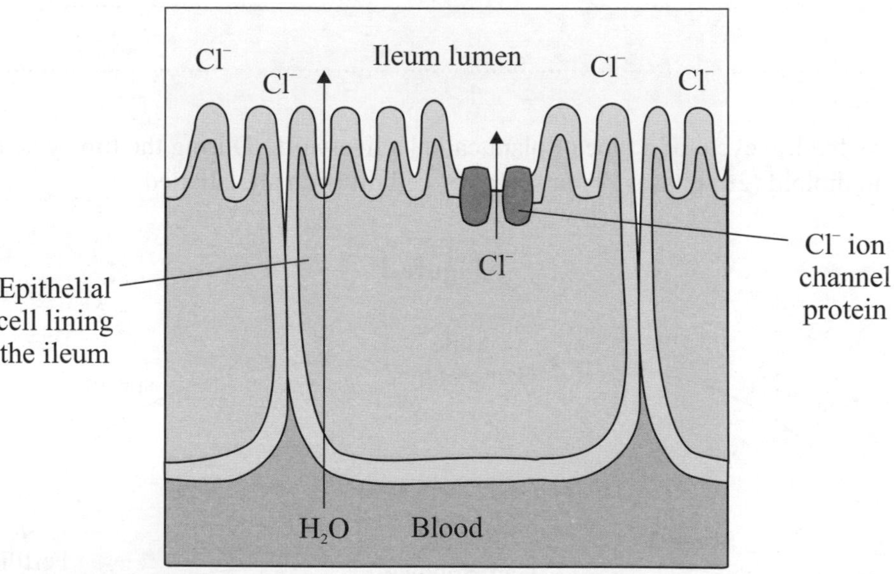


3.1 Use **Figure 3** to explain how cholera causes water to be lost from the blood.

.....................................................................................................................................

.....................................................................................................................................

.....................................................................................................................................

.....................................................................................................................................

.....................................................................................................................................

.....................................................................................................................................

**(4 marks)**

3.2 Suggest **one** structural difference between *V. cholerae* and an ileum epithelial cell.

..........................................................................................................................................

..........................................................................................................................................

**(1 mark)**

3.3 The toxin released by *V. cholerae* is a protein.
It attaches to specific receptor proteins on the surface of the ileum epithelial cells.
Give **one** other example of a pathogen interacting with receptor proteins in the human body.

..........................................................................................................................................

..........................................................................................................................................

**(1 mark)**

3.4 There are several different strains of *V. cholerae*. These are called antigenic variants.
Explain how antigenic variation can allow *V. cholerae* to cause illness in people who have had cholera in the past.

..........................................................................................................................................

..........................................................................................................................................

..........................................................................................................................................

..........................................................................................................................................

**(3 marks)**

Now for a comprehension question — you'll get one just like it in the AS-level Paper 1 exam. In a question like this, it's important to read the passage carefully. I recommend giving it a good read through once in full before you tackle any of the question parts. Then, as you answer the question parts, you can recap the relevant bits of the passage.

4 Read the following passage.

Western blotting is an antibody-based analytical technique that can be used to detect the presence of specific proteins in a sample. It can be used as a diagnostic test for hepatitis B virus (HBV).

To start with, cell fractionation is used to extract proteins from a sample of cells that are known to be infected with HBV. An electric current is then used to separate the proteins out into bands in a block of gel. The protein bands are transferred from the gel to a membrane which has non-specific protein binding sites across its whole surface. The membrane is then incubated with milk so that protein binding sites without bands attached are filled with protein — this is called blocking.

After the blocking step, the membrane is incubated with a blood sample from the patient. If the patient is infected with HBV, antibodies in their blood bind specifically to the bands corresponding to HBV proteins on the membrane. The membrane is then washed and incubated with secondary antibodies that bind specifically to the first antibody. These secondary antibodies have an enzyme attached to them called horseradish peroxidase (HRP). At room temperature and in the presence of its substrate, HRP catalyses a reaction that produces a colour change. This reaction can be used to visualise bands that have antibodies bound to them. If bands are visible after a second washing step, this indicates that the patient is infected with HBV.

Using information from the passage and your own knowledge, answer the following questions.

4.1 Cell fractionation is used to extract proteins from a sample of cells that are known to be infected with HBV (lines 3-4).

Outline how cell fractionation could be used to extract proteins from the cells.

..............................................................................................................

..............................................................................................................

..............................................................................................................

**(2 marks)**

4.2 The process of western blotting requires a blocking step (lines 6-7).

Suggest why this blocking step is needed.

..............................................................................................................

..............................................................................................................

**(1 mark)**

4.3 After the blocking step, the membrane is incubated with a blood sample from the patient. If the patient is infected with HBV, antibodies in their blood bind specifically to the bands corresponding to HBV proteins on the membrane (lines 8-10).

Explain why the blood of a patient with HBV contains antibodies against HBV proteins.

..............................................................................................................

..............................................................................................................

..............................................................................................................

..............................................................................................................

..............................................................................................................

**(3 marks)**

4.4 At room temperature and in the presence of its substrate, HRP catalyses a reaction that produces a colour change (lines 12-13).

Suggest why a higher temperature may not be suitable for this reaction.

..............................................................................................................

..............................................................................................................

**(1 mark)**

4.5 This reaction can be used to visualise bands that have antibodies bound to them (lines 13-14).

Explain why bands would not be observed for an individual who is not infected with HBV.

..............................................................................................................

..............................................................................................................

..............................................................................................................

..............................................................................................................

**(3 marks)**

EXAM TIP

Each of these Mixed Questions requires you to apply your knowledge of several different areas of the specification. It shouldn't come as a surprise that you'll get exam questions that require you to do the same thing. What it boils down to is this — you need to know your stuff inside out and back to front. So if you haven't started already, you'd better get revising.

Score

43

# Answers

## Topic One — Biological Molecules

### Pages 3-4: Biological Molecules — 1

1.1 A molecule made from a large number of monomers joined together ***[1 mark]***.

1.2 E.g.

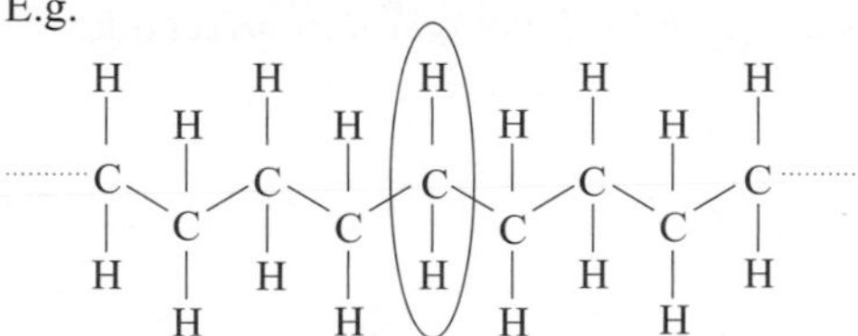

***[1 mark]***

1.3 E.g. monosaccharides, amino acids and nucleotides ***[1 mark]***.

2.1 alpha-glucose/α-glucose ***[1 mark]***

*You must have specified alpha-glucose to get the mark here. Make sure you know the difference between alpha- and beta-glucose.*

2.2 maltose ***[1 mark]***

2.3 A water molecule is used ***[1 mark]*** to break/hydrolyse the glycosidic bond in the disaccharide/maltose ***[1 mark]***. This produces the two monomers/alpha-glucose molecules ***[1 mark]***.

3.1 alpha helix ***[1 mark]***

3.2 Both secondary and tertiary structures contain hydrogen bonds ***[1 mark]***. Tertiary structures also contain ionic bonds and disulfide bridges ***[1 mark]***.

3.3 Enzymes are proteins that catalyse biological reactions ***[1 mark]***. The tertiary structure affects the shape of an enzyme's active site ***[1 mark]***. The shape of the active site needs to be specific to the shape of the substrate to catalyse the reaction ***[1 mark]***.

3.4 It is made up of several different polypeptide chains ***[1 mark]***, held together by bonds ***[1 mark]***.

3.5 A low pH interferes with the bonds in the haemoglobin molecule ***[1 mark]***. This causes its shape to change, so it can no longer bind to oxygen ***[1 mark]***.

### Pages 5-8: Biological Molecules — 2

1.1

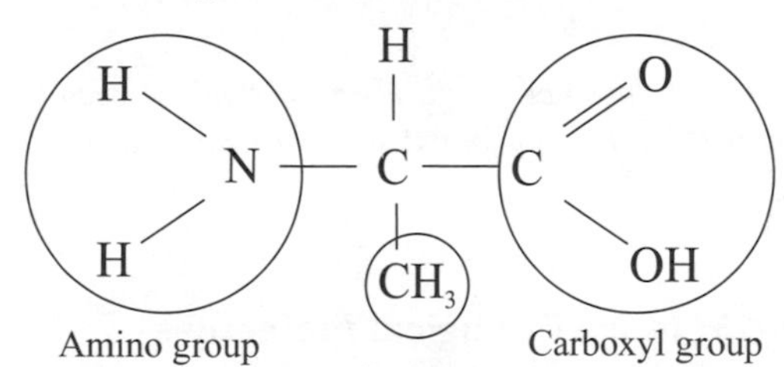


***[1 mark each]***

1.2 It has a different R group ***[1 mark]***.

1.3 E.g.

Peptide bond

***[1 mark for the correct diagram, 1 mark for correctly labelling the peptide bond]***

1.4 water ***[1 mark]***

1.5 The human body contains enzymes (which are not present in the laboratory) ***[1 mark]***. These catalyse the (hydrolysis) reaction that breaks the bond / increase the rate at which the bond is broken down ***[1 mark]***.

2.1 Add Benedict's reagent to the sample and heat in a water bath that has been brought to the boil ***[1 mark]***. A positive result gives a coloured, e.g. yellow/orange/brick-red, precipitate ***[1 mark]***.

2.2

| Sample | Type of carbohydrate present | | |
|---|---|---|---|
| | Reducing sugar | Non-reducing sugar | Starch |
| A | | | |
| B | | | |
| C | | | |

***[2 marks for all three correct, otherwise 1 mark for one or two correct answers]***

2.3 Any one from: e.g. after testing, they could filter the solutions and weigh the precipitates. / After testing, they could observe the difference in the colour of the precipitates (a green/yellow precipitate indicates less reducing sugar is present than an orange/brick-red precipitate). ***[1 mark]***

2.4 glucose and galactose ***[1 mark]***

3.1 phospholipid ***[1 mark]***

3.2 The phospholipid head is hydrophilic ***[1 mark]***, but the phospholipid tail is hydrophobic ***[1 mark]***. The molecules arrange themselves in this way to prevent the hydrophobic tails from coming into contact with the water ***[1 mark]***.

3.3 E.g. they make up cell membranes ***[1 mark]***. The hydrophobic regions act as a barrier to water-soluble substances ***[1 mark]***.

4.1 Fatty acid 2 has a double bond between two carbon atoms, whereas fatty acid 1 does not ***[1 mark]***. This means that the fatty acid 1 is saturated and fatty acid 2 is unsaturated ***[1 mark]***.

4.2 Three fatty acids combine with one glycerol molecule ***[1 mark]*** in a series of three condensation reactions ***[1 mark]***. These form ester bonds between the glycerol and fatty acids ***[1 mark]***.

4.3 E.g. triglycerides are used for storage of energy ***[1 mark]*** because they're insoluble / they contain lots of chemical energy ***[1 mark]***.

4.4 Shake some of the sample to be tested with ethanol until it dissolves, then pour into a test tube of water ***[1 mark]***. If a lipid is present, a white emulsion will form ***[1 mark]***.

4.5 Lipids cannot dissolve in water so if they are present, they form an emulsion ***[1 mark]***.

## Pages 9-12: Biological Molecules — 3

1.1 E.g. it has lots of side branches ***[1 mark]***, meaning stored glucose can be released quickly ***[1 mark]***.

*Remember, glycogen is the main energy storage molecule in animals.*

1.2 E.g.

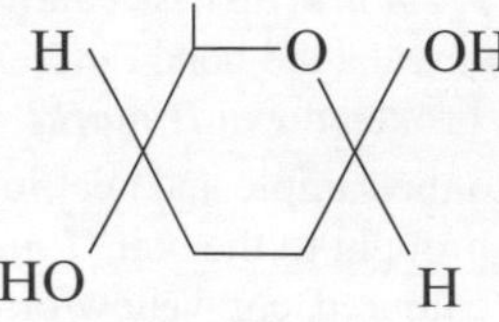


***[1 mark]***

In alpha-glucose the OH/hydroxyl group and the H/hydrogen on the right-hand side are reversed ***[1 mark]***.

*You could have drawn the full skeletal formula for beta-glucose here instead.*

1.3 It allows cellulose molecules to form strong fibres/microfibrils ***[1 mark]***, which provide structural support/support the cell wall ***[1 mark]***.

1.4 Advantage: e.g. it is more compact ***[1 mark]***. Disadvantage: e.g. it can't be broken down as quickly ***[1 mark]***.

2.1 At low temperatures, the rate of the reaction is slow because the kinetic energy of the enzyme and substrate molecules is low ***[1 mark]***. As temperature increases to the optimum, the rate increases as there are more successful collisions between enzymes and substrate molecules ***[1 mark]***. At temperatures higher than the optimum, the rate decreases as the enzyme is denatured ***[1 mark]***.

2.2 Enzyme B because it has the higher optimum temperature ***[1 mark]***, which will allow it to function at the higher temperatures found in a tropical climate ***[1 mark]***.

2.3 The rate of reaction would be lower across the whole temperature range ***[1 mark]***.

2.4 The insecticide molecule is a similar shape to enzyme A's substrate ***[1 mark]***. The insecticide molecule occupies enzyme A's active site ***[1 mark]*** so the substrate cannot fit and the respiration reaction cannot be catalysed ***[1 mark]***. This interrupts the respiration process and kills the insect ***[1 mark]***.

3.1 Add a few drops of sodium hydroxide to a solution of the sample ***[1 mark]***, then a few drops of copper (II) sulfate solution ***[1 mark]***. A colour change from blue to purple/lilac is a positive result ***[1 mark]***.

3.2 Its parallel chains and cross linkages make it physically strong ***[1 mark]***.

3.3 E.g. Protein B: an enzyme ***[1 mark]***. Protein C: an antibody ***[1 mark]***.

*Enzymes are usually proteins that are roughly spherical, so B could be an enzyme. The two light and two heavy polypeptide chains are typical of an antibody, so C is likely to be an antibody.*

3.4 Channel proteins transport molecules and ions across cell membranes ***[1 mark]***. The hydrophobic regions are repelled by water and the hydrophilic regions are attracted to it ***[1 mark]***. This causes the protein to fold up and form a channel through the membrane (through which water soluble molecules can pass) ***[1 mark]***.

4.1 The independent variable is enzyme concentration and the dependent variable is the volume of oxygen produced ***[1 mark]***.

4.2 ± 0.5 $cm^3$ ***[1 mark]***

4.3 E.g. collected the gas in a measuring cylinder with a smaller resolution ***[1 mark]***.

4.4 Rate = $\frac{17}{20}$

$= \mathbf{0.85\ cm^3\ s^{-1}}$

***[1 mark for 0.85, 1 mark for the correct units]***

4.5

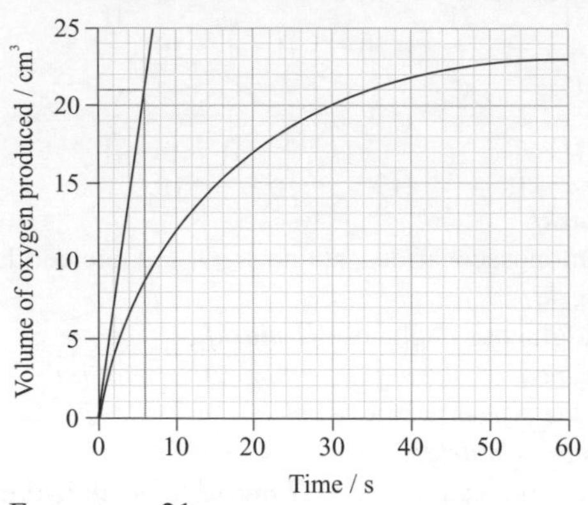


E.g. rate = $\frac{21}{6.0}$

$= \mathbf{3.5\ cm^3\ s^{-1}}$

***[1 mark, accept anything from 3.2 $cm^3\ s^{-1}$ to 3.8 $cm^3\ s^{-1}$]***

*Tangents can be tricky things to draw accurately so the examiners will usually accept answers that are a bit below or a bit above what they got themselves — even so, try to draw your line as carefully as you can.*

4.6 E.g.

***[1 mark]***

*Don't worry if your line's not exactly like this. You just need to make sure it's steeper than the original but still starts and plateaus at the same values.*

## Pages 13-15: More Biological Molecules

1.1 E.g. it is involved in the co-transport of glucose/amino acids across cell membranes ***[1 mark]***.

1.2 E.g. a higher concentration of hydrogen ions lowers the pH ***[1 mark]***, so the internal environment becomes more acidic ***[1 mark]***.

1.3 Nitrate ions contain nitrogen/N ***[1 mark]*** which forms part of the organic base in DNA ***[1 mark]***.

2.1 Because water has a high latent heat of vaporisation ***[1 mark]***, a lot of energy is removed from the kangaroo's body when the water in the saliva evaporates from its forearms ***[1 mark]***. This reduces the kangaroo's body temperature ***[1 mark]***.

2.2 Water has a high specific heat capacity ***[1 mark]***, which means it doesn't heat up as quickly as the air ***[1 mark]***.

2.3 There is strong cohesion between water molecules ***[1 mark]***. This allows water to travel in a column up the xylem/tube-like transport cells in a tree trunk ***[1 mark]***.

3.1 phosphodiester bond ***[1 mark]***

3.2 condensation reaction ***[1 mark]***

3.3 The molecule contains uracil/U bases (in place of thymine/T bases) ***[1 mark]***.

3.4 Complementary/specific base pairing ***[1 mark]*** means that hydrogen bonds will form between the base pairs A and U, and C and G ***[1 mark]***. Because the two halves of the RNA sequence are complementary, it causes the RNA strand to fold into a stem-loop structure ***[1 mark]***.

4.1 DNA helicase separates the nucleotide strands / causes the DNA helix to unwind ***[1 mark]*** by breaking the hydrogen bonds between bases ***[1 mark]***. DNA polymerase joins the nucleotides in the new DNA strand together ***[1 mark]*** by catalysing condensation reactions between the nucleotides ***[1 mark]***.

4.2 It is known as a nucleotide derivative because it has a similar structure to a(n) (adenine) nucleotide ***[1 mark]*** but it has been modified with the addition of two more phosphate groups ***[1 mark]***.

4.3 It catalyses the breakdown of ATP ***[1 mark]*** into ADP and inorganic phosphate ***[1 mark]***.

4.4 The results show that DNA replication will not occur in the absence of ATP or when ATP hydrolase is inactive ***[1 mark]***. This indicates that the breakdown of ATP (by ATP hydrolase) is essential for DNA replication ***[1 mark]***. A possible explanation is that DNA replication requires energy and/or inorganic phosphate released by the breakdown of ATP ***[1 mark]***.

## Topic Two — Cells

### Pages 16-18: Cell Structure and Division — 1

1.1 The student could have placed the root tip on a microscope slide and cut 2 mm/a small section from the very tip of it ***[1 mark]***. Then used a mounted needle to break the tip open and spread the cells out thinly ***[1 mark]***. Then added a few drops of stain, e.g. ethano-orcein or toluidine blue O, and left it for a few minutes ***[1 mark]***. Then placed a cover slip over the cells and pushed down firmly ***[1 mark]***.

1.2 Any two from: e.g. worn goggles/gloves / taken care with glass beakers/slides/cover slips / taken care with sharp tools. ***[1 mark for each correct answer]***

1.3 Root tips are actively growing so the cells here will be undergoing mitosis/dividing ***[1 mark]***.

1.4 E.g. if a cell contains visible chromosomes this indicates that it is dividing ***[1 mark]***.

1.5 $\text{mitotic index} = \frac{\text{number of cells with visible chromosomes}}{\text{total number of cells observed}}$

80 + 240 = 320 cells in total

240 ÷ 320 = **0.75**

***[2 marks for the correct answer, otherwise 1 mark for the correct working]***

2.1 E.g. because electron microscopes have a higher resolution ***[1 mark]*** so they can be used to look at smaller objects (like bacteria) in more detail ***[1 mark]***.

2.2 A transmission electron microscope/TEM ***[1 mark]***. E.g. transmission electron micrographs show a 2D cross section through a sample as seen in Figure 1 ***[1 mark]***.

2.3 Any two from: e.g. a prokaryotic cell is smaller than a eukaryotic cell. / There is no nucleus present in a prokaryotic cell. / A prokaryotic cell contains no membrane-bound organelles. / Ribosomes are smaller in a prokaryotic cell than in a eukaryotic cell. / The DNA in a prokaryotic cell is circular, not linear. / A prokaryotic cell may contain plasmids. ***[2 marks]***

2.4 Human cells have no cell wall, so the drugs will have no effect on them ***[1 mark]***.

2.5 WNV has an attachment protein on its surface ***[1 mark]*** which binds to the complementary $\alpha_v\beta_3$ integrin present on human cells ***[1 mark]***. If $\alpha_v\beta_3$ integrin isn't functioning on human cells, WNV wouldn't be able to invade and reproduce inside these cells ***[1 mark]***.

3.1 Similarities: any one from: e.g. a sperm cell and a bacterial cell can both have a flagellum ***[1 mark]***. / A sperm cell and a bacterial cell both have a cell membrane ***[1 mark]***.
Differences: any one from: e.g. a sperm cell has a nucleus but a bacterial cell has circular DNA floating freely in the cytoplasm ***[1 mark]***. / A bacterial cell has a cell wall but a sperm cell only has a cell membrane ***[1 mark]***.
***[Maximum 2 marks available]***

3.2 The flagellum requires ATP to move, which is generated by mitochondria ***[1 mark]***.

3.3 E.g. a transmission/scanning electron microscope ***[1 mark]*** because these have a higher resolution than light microscopes, which would be needed to study the internal detail of mitochondria ***[1 mark]***.

3.4 As the function of sperm is to deliver the genetic material to the egg, it isn't necessary for it to make lots of proteins for cell growth and repair / having lots of organelles may reduce its motility ***[1 mark]***. A mitotic body cell is undergoing mitosis/division ***[1 mark]***, so it requires ribosomes for cell growth prior to division ***[1 mark]***.

### Pages 19-21: Cell Structure and Division — 2

1.1 A cell that carries out a particular function ***[1 mark]***.

1.2 E.g. each cell would only contain one nucleus. / Each nucleus would contain the same amount of genetic material. ***[1 mark]***

1.3 The role of cell type A is to ingest invading pathogens because a greater percentage of the cell contains lysosomes than cell type B ***[1 mark]***. Lysosomes are necessary to digest pathogens once they have been ingested by the cell ***[1 mark]***. The role of cell type B is to secrete enzymes because a greater percentage of the cell contains rough endoplasmic reticulum than cell type A ***[1 mark]***. This organelle is covered with ribosomes which synthesise proteins, such as enzymes / is responsible for folding and processing proteins, such as enzymes ***[1 mark]***.

1.4 E.g. chloroplasts contain thylakoid membranes/grana, whereas mitochondria contain a folded membrane that form structures called cristae ***[1 mark]*** / Chloroplasts are the site of photosynthesis, whereas mitochondria are the site of aerobic respiration ***[1 mark]***.

2.1 Any five from: clip the slide onto the stage ***[1 mark]***. Select the lowest-powered objective lens ***[1 mark]***. Use the coarse adjustment knob to bring the stage up to just below the objective lens ***[1 mark]***. Look down the eyepiece and use the coarse adjustment knob to move the stage down until the image is roughly in focus ***[1 mark]***. Adjust the focus with the fine adjustment knob until you get a clear image of what's on the slide ***[1 mark]***. If a greater magnification is required, refocus using a higher-powered objective lens ***[1 mark]***.
***[Maximum of 5 marks available]***

2.2 One division of the stage micrometer is the same as four eyepiece divisions.
0.1 mm ÷ 4 = 0.025 mm
0.025 mm × 1000 = **25 μm**
***[2 marks for the correct answer, otherwise 1 mark for the correct working]***

2.3 The stage micrometer will appear larger, so each eyepiece division will be a smaller measurement ***[1 mark]***.

2.4 E.g. length of cell = 36 mm
36 mm × 1000 = 36 000 μm
object size = image size ÷ magnification
= 36 000 μm ÷ 100
= **360 μm**
***[accept values between 350 μm and 370 μm, 2 marks for the correct answer, otherwise 1 mark for the correct working]***

3.1 The production of ATP ***[1 mark]***.

3.2 Abnormal mitochondria might not produce as much ATP as normal mitochondria ***[1 mark]***. This means the heart tissue may not have sufficient energy to work properly/for muscle contraction ***[1 mark]***.

3.3 inner membrane ***[1 mark]***

3.4 E.g. abnormal mice have smaller mitochondria/fewer cristae ***[1 mark]***. This will reduce the surface area of the mitochondria and reduces ATP production ***[1 mark]***. Abnormal mice have mitochondria with a less dense matrix ***[1 mark]***. The matrix contains the enzymes needed for aerobic respiration, so this will also impair ATP production ***[1 mark]***.

3.5 Object size = 1.5 μm ÷ 1000
= 0.0015 mm
magnification = image size ÷ object size
= 29 mm ÷ 0.0015 mm
= **× 19 333**
***[accept values between × 18 667 and × 20 000, 2 marks for the correct answer, otherwise 1 mark for using the correct rearrangement of the magnification formula]***

## Pages 22-25: Cell Structure and Division — 3

1.1 E.g. they could add a buffer solution to the sample ***[1 mark]*** and grind the cells in a blender ***[1 mark]***. They could then filter the solution to remove the cell and tissue debris ***[1 mark]***.

1.2 At lower temperatures the activity of enzymes that break down organelles is reduced ***[1 mark]***.

1.3

| Contents of pellet | Sequence of Separation |
|---|---|
| Mitochondria and chloroplasts | 2 |
| Nuclei | 1 |
| Ribosomes | 4 |
| Endoplasmic reticulum | 3 |

***[1 mark]***

1.4 It contains chloroplasts, which are responsible for photosynthesis, so would not be needed by root cells ***[1 mark]***.

1.5 Ribosomes are made in the nucleolus ***[1 mark]***. The nucleolus is found within the nucleus ***[1 mark]***. If there was reduced function of the nuclear pore complexes, then fewer ribosomes could pass through the nuclear pore into the cytoplasm ***[1 mark]***.

2.1 Both replicate inside a host cell ***[1 mark]***. Both can cause a cell to burst (lysis) and release infective bodies ***[1 mark]***. Viruses replicate by injecting their DNA or RNA into a host cell, whereas bacteria, such as *C. trachomatis*, replicate by binary fission/cell division ***[1 mark]***.

2.2 E.g. the inhibition of ribosomes by azithromycin means that bacteria can't synthesise proteins ***[1 mark]***. Protein synthesis is needed for mitosis/cell division, so the drug prevents bacteria multiplying ***[1 mark]***.

2.3 Viruses don't have ribosomes ***[1 mark]***.

2.4 During replication, plasmids can be replicated many times and can be shared unequally between the daughter cells ***[1 mark]***. This means that the daughter cells can have a different number of plasmids, and therefore relative DNA content, to the parent cell and to each other ***[1 mark]***.

3.1 Metaphase ***[1 mark]***. The chromosomes are lined up along the middle of the cell ***[1 mark]***.

3.2 A peak in the concentration of cyclin E occurs when the mass of DNA starts to increase ***[1 mark]***. This suggests that cyclin E may trigger DNA replication in the cell / entry into the S stage of interphase ***[1 mark]***. The peak in the concentration of cyclin B is followed by a decrease/halving in the mass of DNA ***[1 mark]***. This suggests that cyclin B may trigger the cell to enter the mitosis stage ***[1 mark]***.

4.1 DNA synthesis is needed to double the genetic content of the cell before it divides ***[1 mark]***.

4.2 Because chemotherapy aims to reduce/control the rate of cell division in dividing cells ***[1 mark]*** and other non-cancerous body cells don't divide as often as hair follicle cells ***[1 mark]***.

4.3 $\text{mitotic index} = \dfrac{\text{number of cells dividing}}{\text{total number of cells observed}}$
number of cells dividing = 0.9 × 200
= **180 cells**
***[2 marks for the correct answer, otherwise 1 mark for using the correct formula]***

4.4 The chromosomes would not line up in the middle of the cell and attach to the spindle fibres *[1 mark]*. This could mean that there isn't separation of the sister chromatids, and could result in there being an incorrect amount of genetic material in each daughter cell/mitosis would not progress to anaphase *[1 mark]*. This disruption of the cell cycle would kill the cancerous cells *[1 mark]*.

## Pages 26-28: Cell Membranes — 1

1.1 Proteins are scattered amongst the phospholipids, like tiles in a mosaic *[1 mark]*. The phospholipids are constantly moving, so the structure is fluid *[1 mark]*.

1.2 The cholesterol molecules would restrict the movement of the phospholipids *[1 mark]*, making the structure less fluid and more rigid *[1 mark]*.

1.3 E.g. the cell-surface membranes are likely to have a high proportion of carrier or channel proteins *[1 mark]* in order to carry nutrients via facilitated diffusion or active transport *[1 mark]*. The cell-surface membrane is likely to have a large surface area/microvilli *[1 mark]* to maximise the rate of absorption of nutrients *[1 mark]*.

1.4 E.g. a large number of carrier or channel proteins *[1 mark]* in order to allow cations to cross the cell membrane quickly *[1 mark]*.

2.1 B *[1 mark]*

2.2 Phospholipids have a hydrophobic tail and a hydrophilic head *[1 mark]*. The hydrophilic heads are attracted to the water molecules in the cytoplasm or cell surroundings *[1 mark]*, and the hydrophobic tails are repelled from them, so a bilayer is formed *[1 mark]*.

2.3 The water will move from the exterior to the interior of the cell *[1 mark]* because the water potential of the exterior is higher/less negative than the water potential of the interior *[1 mark]*.

3 Any five from: e.g. sodium ions are actively transported out of the ileum epithelial cells into the blood *[1 mark]* by the sodium-potassium pump *[1 mark]*. This creates a concentration gradient of sodium ions between the lumen of the ileum and the interior of the epithelial cells *[1 mark]*. Sodium ions diffuse down this concentration gradient into the epithelial cells *[1 mark]* via sodium-glucose co-transporter proteins *[1 mark]*. The co-transporter proteins transport glucose into the cells along with the sodium ions *[1 mark]*.

4.1 To make sure any betalains/pigments released by the cutting of the beetroot were washed away *[1 mark]*.

4.2 Colorimetry analysis of distilled water *[1 mark]*.

4.3 Any four from: e.g. increasing the temperature from 20 °C to 40 °C increases the fluidity of the phospholipids in the beetroot cell membranes *[1 mark]*. At temperatures above 40 °C, the membrane starts to break down / proteins in the membrane start to denature *[1 mark]*. The membrane surrounding the vacuole therefore becomes more permeable with increasing temperature *[1 mark]*, meaning that betalains/pigments leak out into the distilled water *[1 mark]*. The more pigments released, the higher the absorbance reading *[1 mark]*.

4.4 Cell membranes contain channel proteins and carrier proteins *[1 mark]*. Proteins are denatured by extremes of pH / extremes of pH interfere with the bonding in proteins, causing them to change shape *[1 mark]*. If the proteins are not able to function and control what goes in or out of the cell, membrane permeability will increase *[1 mark]*.

## Pages 29-30: Cell Membranes — 2

1.1

| Concentration of sucrose solution to be made up / mol dm$^{-3}$ | Volume of 1 mol dm$^{-3}$ sucrose solution used / cm$^3$ | Volume of water used / cm$^3$ | Final volume of solution to be made up / cm$^3$ |
|---|---|---|---|
| 1 | 20 | 0 | 20 |
| 0.75 | 15 | **5** | 20 |
| 0.5 | **10** | **10** | 20 |
| 0.25 | **5** | **15** | 20 |
| 0 | **0** | **20** | 20 |

***[2 marks for all 5 rows correct, otherwise 1 mark for 4 rows correct]***

1.2 Any two from: e.g. the temperature the potato samples were incubated at / the length of time the potato samples were incubated for / the volume of sucrose solution used / the variety of potato used / the age of potato used. *[2 marks]*

1.3 The line of best fit crosses the $x$-axis of Figure 1 halfway between 0.25 and 0.50, so the sucrose concentration of potato cells = approximately 0.375 mol dm$^{-3}$.
A 0.3 mol dm$^{-3}$ sucrose solution has a water potential of –850 kPa. A 0.4 mol dm$^{-3}$ sucrose solution has a water potential of –1130 kPa.
So a 0.375 mol dm$^{-3}$ sucrose solution has a water potential of approximately:
(–1130) – (–850) = 280 × 0.75 = 210
–850 – 210 = **–1060 kPa**
***[2 marks for an answer > –850 and < –1130 kPa, otherwise 1 mark for estimating the sucrose concentration of the potato cells to be between 0.3 and 0.4 mol dm$^{-3}$]***

1.4 The sweet potato tissue is likely to have a lower water potential than that of the white potato *[1 mark]* because it is likely to have a higher sucrose concentration *[1 mark]*.

*The extra sucrose (with some other sugars too) is what makes the sweet potato sweet.*

2.1 ATP is made inside the cell, rather than outside it, so the ATP binding site has to face inwards *[1 mark]*.

2.2 To catalyse the hydrolysis of ATP (into ADP and $P_i$) *[1 mark]* in order to release energy for the active transport of the calcium ions *[1 mark]*.

2.3 $Ca^{2+}$ ions carry a charge, making them water soluble/hydrophilic *[1 mark]*. This makes it difficult for them to travel directly through the hydrophobic centre of the phospholipid bilayer *[1 mark]*.

## Pages 31-34: Cells and the Immune System — 1

1.1 A protein that binds to a specific antigen ***[1 mark]***.

1.2 B-cells/B-lymphocytes / plasma cells ***[1 mark]***

1.3 It has four variable regions, which form the antigen-binding sites ***[1 mark]***. The tertiary structure of the variable regions varies between antibodies ***[1 mark]***, giving the binding sites of each antibody a specific shape that is complementary to a specific antigen ***[1 mark]***.

1.4 E.g. it allows the antibody to bind to more antigens at once ***[1 mark]***, so there is a greater chance of agglutination occurring / more pathogens can be phagocytosed at once ***[1 mark]***.

1.5 $2000 \times 60 \times 60 = 7200000$ ***[1 mark]***
$= \mathbf{7.2 \times 10^6}$ ***[1 mark]***

*There are 60 seconds in a minute and 60 minutes in an hour. So, to work out how many molecules could be produced in an hour, multiply the number that can be produced in one second by 60, and then by 60 again.*

2.1 Any two from: e.g. their age. / Their ethnicity. / Their sex. / If they are generally healthy/have a disease. / If they are currently taking any medication. / If they have previously been infected with the virus. ***[2 marks]***

2.2 $\text{percentage change} = \frac{\text{final value} - \text{original value}}{\text{original value}} \times 100$

$((90 - 10) \div 10) \times 100 = \mathbf{800\%}$ ***[1 mark]***

2.3 It means that there is a greater than 5% probability that the results are due to chance ***[1 mark]***, so there is no significant difference between the means ***[1 mark]***.

2.4 The children who aren't vaccinated can be protected through herd immunity ***[1 mark]***. If enough people are immune to a pathogen, it won't be able to spread easily through a population (even if not everyone is immune/has been vaccinated) ***[1 mark]***.

2.5 Antigen variability means that a pathogen's antigens can change ***[1 mark]***. If antigens change, memory cells produced as a result of a vaccine won't recognise them ***[1 mark]***. Therefore, there won't be a fast secondary response to the pathogen / the person won't be immune to the pathogen ***[1 mark]***.

3.1 E.g.

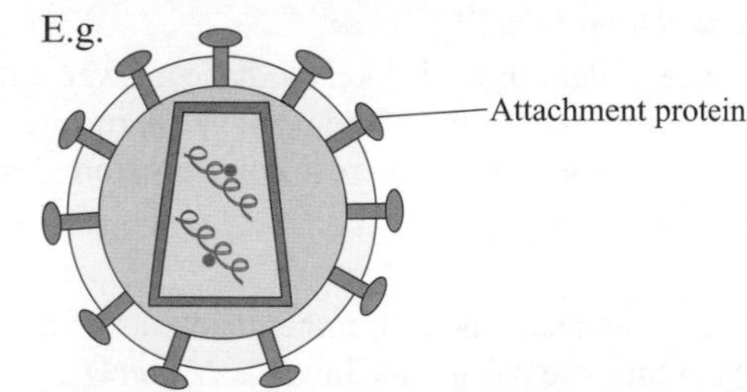


***[1 mark]***

3.2 The attachment proteins on the virus have a specific tertiary structure ***[1 mark]*** which allows them to bind to the complementary CD4 cell-surface receptor ***[1 mark]***, but not any other receptors/membrane proteins ***[1 mark]***.

3.3 The HTLV-I genetic material is RNA ***[1 mark]***. Once inside the cell, reverse transcriptase is used to make a complementary DNA copy of the viral RNA ***[1 mark]***. From this, double-stranded DNA is made and inserted into the T-cell DNA ***[1 mark]***. The T-cell enzymes are then used to make HTLV-I proteins from the viral DNA, including Tax ***[1 mark]***.

4.1 ELISA/enzyme-linked immunosorbent assay ***[1 mark]***

4.2 Only antibodies that are complementary to the *Leishmania* antigen can bind to it ***[1 mark]***.

4.3 To remove any unbound antibodies ***[1 mark]*** so that they don't affect the result / cause a false positive result ***[1 mark]***.

4.4 The enzyme catalyses the reaction of solution X/its substrate, causing a colour change that indicates a positive result ***[1 mark]***.

4.5 E.g. individuals may see colour change differently. / Colour change may be hard to detect by eye. ***[1 mark]***

4.6 E.g. colorimetry ***[1 mark]***

## Pages 35-38: Cells and the Immune System — 2

1.1

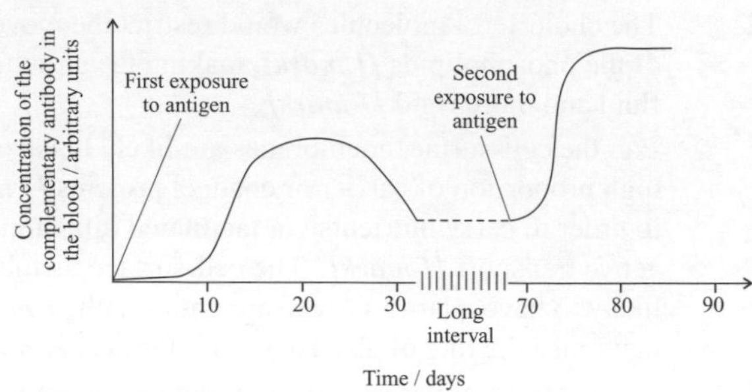


***[1 mark]***

*A second exposure to the same antigen will always produce a quicker response, with a greater concentration of complementary antibodies.*

1.2 E.g. the antibody concentration remains low for several days after exposure to the antigen because there aren't many B-cells that can produce the complementary antibody ***[1 mark]***. Antibody concentration increases as activated B-cells divide to produce plasma cells, which start to rapidly produce lots of antibodies ***[1 mark]***. Antibody concentration reaches a gradual peak and then falls as plasma cells die off ***[1 mark]***. It doesn't fall back to pre-exposure levels because memory cells remain in the body ***[1 mark]***.

2.1 E.g. so that the woman produces antibodies against the bacteria, which would be transferred to her baby (via the placenta) before it is born ***[1 mark]***.

2.2 Any five from: e.g. the vaccine contains GBS antigens ***[1 mark]***. Antigen-presenting cells present these antigens to helper T-cells ***[1 mark]***. When the antigens bind to receptors on helper T-cell membranes, the helper T-cells are activated ***[1 mark]***. The helper T-cells then activate B-cells ***[1 mark]***, which divide to produce plasma cells that secrete antibodies against GBS ***[1 mark]***. The activated T-cells and B-cells both produce memory cells ***[1 mark]***. Memory cells remain in the body for a long time and result in a faster response to GBS antigens if they appear in the body again ***[1 mark]***.
***[Maximum of 5 marks available]***

2.3 Any two from: e.g. the immunity the baby receives from its mother is immediate, whereas immunity from a vaccine takes time to develop. / A vaccine involves exposing the baby to an antigen, whereas breastfeeding provides immunity without needing to expose the baby to an antigen. / The baby does not produce memory cells as a result of breastfeeding, but memory cells are produced as a result of a vaccine. / The immunity the baby gets from breastfeeding only lasts for a short time, whereas the immunity from a vaccine lasts much longer.
***[2 marks]***

2.4 Viruses do not have cell walls ***[1 mark]***.

3.1 E.g. the monoclonal antibodies bind to the (beta-amyloid) proteins in the plaque and form antigen-antibody complexes ***[1 mark]***. This labels the proteins for destruction by phagocytosis, which breaks down the plaque ***[1 mark]***.

3.2 The vehicle acted as a control ***[1 mark]*** so that the scientists could ensure that the drug caused the observed effect on plaque number and not the vehicle itself ***[1 mark]***.

3.3 Any one from: e.g. gantenerumab cleared plaques that were less than 300 $\mu m^2$ in size. / Compared to the vehicle/control, gantenerumab reduced the number of plaques formed that were less than 600 $\mu m^2$ in size. / Gantenerumab had no effect on plaques that were greater than 600 $\mu m^2$ in size. ***[1 mark]***

*If the number of plaques in treated mice was less than the baseline, then you can conclude that the drug prevented plaque formation and removed some plaques. If it was less than the control but not the baseline, then the drug reduced the number of new plaques formed but didn't remove any.*

3.4 Any four from: e.g. because the study was carried out in mice, not humans, so you don't know how effective the drug would be in humans ***[1 mark]***. The data shows how the drug affected the number of beta-amyloid plaques, not how it affected the symptoms of Alzheimer's ***[1 mark]***. Scientists don't know for certain that amyloid plaques cause Alzheimer's ***[1 mark]***. The gantenerumab did not remove all the plaques in the mice's brains ***[1 mark]***. The data does not record any side effects experienced by the mice, which might make the drug a less effective medical treatment ***[1 mark]***. ***[Maximum of 4 marks available]***

4.1 Different blood types have red blood cells with different antigens ***[1 mark]***. The immune system of someone receiving the wrong blood type would not recognise the antigens on the donated red blood cells / would view the antigens on the donated red blood cells as foreign ***[1 mark]***. This would stimulate an immune response, destroying the blood cells ***[1 mark]***.

4.2 Any six from: e.g. phagocytes recognise foreign antigens on type B red blood cells and engulf them ***[1 mark]***. They present the antigens on their surface ***[1 mark]***. Receptors on helper T-cells bind to these antigens ***[1 mark]***. This stimulates the helper T-cells to activate more phagocytes/cytotoxic T-cells to kill the type B red blood cells ***[1 mark]***. The helper T-cells also activate B-cells ***[1 mark]*** which divide to produce plasma cells that secrete antibodies against the type B antigens ***[1 mark]***. The antibodies bind to the type B antigens causing the type B blood cells to clump together/agglutinate ***[1 mark]***, labelling them for destruction by phagocytosis ***[1 mark]***. ***[Maximum of 6 marks available.]***

4.3 Blood type O has no antigens, so no immune response will be triggered ***[1 mark]***.

4.4 E.g. monoclonal antibodies specific to the antigen(s) of one blood type could be added to a sample of the person's blood ***[1 mark]***. If agglutination is observed, then it can be concluded that the person has that blood type ***[1 mark]***.

# Topic Three — Exchange and Transport

## Pages 39-42: Exchange and Transport Systems — 1

1.1 lamella ***[1 mark]***

1.2 An arrow drawn across structure A in the opposite direction to the arrow showing water flow across the gill filament, e.g.

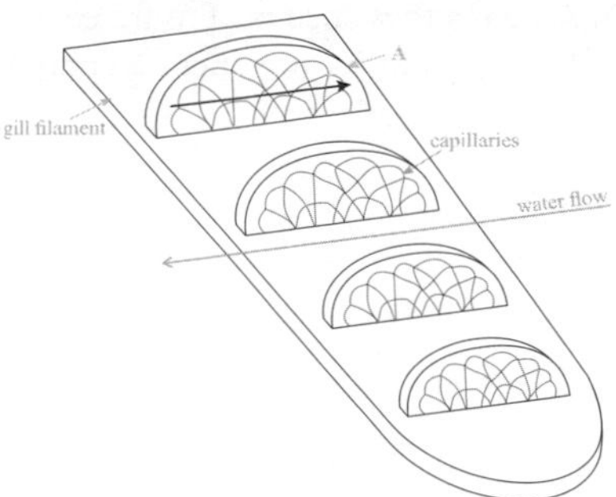


***[1 mark]***

*Fish gills have a counter-current system, meaning the blood flows in the opposite direction to the water.*

1.3 E.g.

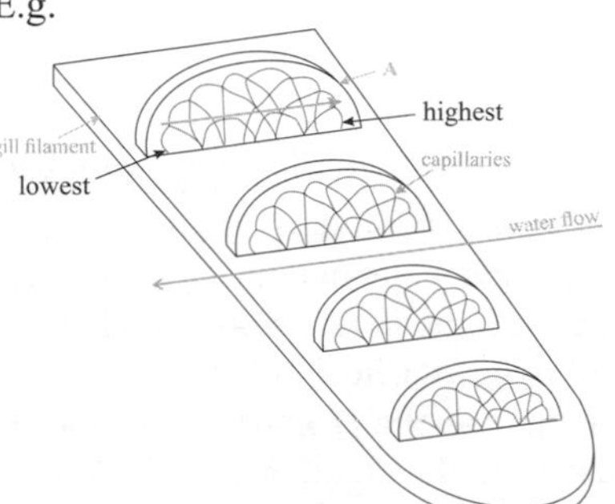


***[1 mark]***

1.4 E.g. the many lamellae give the gill a large surface area ***[1 mark]***, increasing the rate of diffusion of gases ***[1 mark]***.

2.1 E.g. dissecting scissors ***[1 mark]***

2.2 A: spiracle ***[1 mark]***
B: tracheae ***[1 mark]***

2.3 E.g. pipette a drop of water onto a slide ***[1 mark]***. Use tweezers to place a section of structures B/the tracheae onto the drop of water ***[1 mark]***. Stand a cover slip upright on the slide, next to the water drop, then carefully tilt and lower it so it covers the specimen ***[1 mark]***.

2.4 Any two from: e.g. it is able to close its spiracles when it is losing too much water ***[1 mark]***. / It has a waterproof, waxy cuticle all over its body ***[1 mark]***. / It has tiny hairs around the spiracles ***[1 mark]***.

3.1 Mean number of stomata per 0.025 $mm^2$ =
$(5 + 6 + 7 + 4 + 3 + 8 + 5 + 5 + 3 + 4) \div 10 =$
$50 \div 10 = 5$
$150\ mm^2 \div 0.025\ mm^2 = 6000$
Number of stomata you'd expect to find in 150 $mm^2$ =
$5 \times 6000 =$ **30 000 stomata**
***[2 marks for correct answer, otherwise 1 mark for mean per 0.025 mm² = 5, or 1 mark for multiplying mean by 6000]***

3.2 E.g. it is based on data from the lower epidermis only and stomata might not be evenly distributed across a leaf ***[1 mark]***. It is based on a small sample size ***[1 mark]***.

3.3 Mesophyll ***[1 mark]***

3.4 The stoma is sunken in a pit ***[1 mark]***, which traps moist air, reducing the concentration gradient of water between the leaf and the air ***[1 mark]***. This reduces the diffusion and evaporation of water from the leaf ***[1 mark]***.

4.1 *Lepus othus*. Having shorter ears gives the hare a smaller surface area to volume ratio ***[1 mark]***, which means it loses heat less easily ***[1 mark]***. This makes the hare better adapted to surviving at low temperatures ***[1 mark]***.

4.2 Alaskan hares are likely to have a higher metabolic rate than polar bears because hares are smaller ***[1 mark]***, so they have a higher surface area compared to their volume ***[1 mark]***. This means they lose heat more easily, so need a high metabolic rate in order to generate enough heat to stay warm ***[1 mark]***.

5.1

Oxygen concentration

Water

(Blood)

Distance along lamella ***[1 mark]***

5.2 In the parallel flow system, the oxygen concentration gradient between the water and the blood decreases with distance along the lamella ***[1 mark]***, which will mean that the rate of oxygen diffusion will also decrease with distance along the lamella ***[1 mark]***. This means that less oxygen diffuses into the blood than with a counter-current system, where the concentration gradient (and therefore rate of diffusion) is maintained ***[1 mark]***.

## Pages 43-45: Exchange and Transport Systems — 2

1 Bacterium B: 84 ÷ 22 = 3.8181..., so 84 : 22 = 3.81 : 1
Bacterium C: 15.75 ÷ 3.5 = 4.5, so 15.75 : 3.5 = 4.5 : 1
Bacterium with fastest gas exchange: Bacterium **A**
***[1 mark for bacterium A, 1 mark for correct conversion of ratios]***

*Converting all the ratios into the form n : 1 makes it easier to see that Bacterium A has a bigger surface area compared to its volume, which means there is a larger surface for gases to diffuse across. This means the rate of gas exchange can be faster.*

2.1 diaphragm ***[1 mark]***, external intercostal muscles ***[1 mark]***

*You must specify the external intercostal muscles to get the mark here. The internal intercostal muscles only contract during forced expiration.*

2.2 0-2 seconds ***[1 mark]*** because this is when the pressure inside the lungs/the intrapulmonary pressure is negative ***[1 mark]***. Air travels down a pressure gradient, so air must be being taken into the lungs at this point ***[1 mark]***.

2.3 3 seconds ***[1 mark]***

*Lung volume will be smallest when the pressure is highest (and the person is expiring).*

3.1 Any two from: e.g. the alveolar epithelium is only one cell thick ***[1 mark]***. / Alveolar epithelial cells are flat ***[1 mark]***. / Alveoli have a large surface area for gas exchange to take place over ***[1 mark]***.

3.2 Air flow into the emphysema patient's lungs is not restricted, so the inspiration line is relatively normal ***[1 mark]***. The alveoli of the person with emphysema cannot recoil to expel air as well as those of the healthy person however, because of the loss of elastin in the alveoli walls ***[1 mark]***. This limits/slows the flow of air out of the lungs, so the expiration line is lower and more concave ***[1 mark]***.

3.3 1 $dm^3$ = 1000 $cm^3$
So 7.60 $dm^3$ = 7.60 × 1000 = 7600 $cm^3$
Volume of air in each breath = PVR ÷ breaths per minute
= 7600 ÷ 16
= **475 $cm^3$**
***[2 marks for the correct answer, otherwise 1 mark for 4.75 $dm^3$ or for a correct conversion from $dm^3$ to $cm^3$.]***

4.1 E.g. the scar tissue means that the lungs are less able to expand, so they can't hold as much air ***[1 mark]***. To take in enough oxygen, the person has to breathe more quickly ***[1 mark]***.

4.2 Any four from: e.g. the number of annual deaths from asbestosis increased after the ban in 1999, suggesting that the ban was not very effective ***[1 mark]***. (However) it cannot be concluded that the ban was unsuccessful ***[1 mark]***. We don't know whether the increase in deaths would have been greater without the ban ***[1 mark]***. Asbestosis might not develop until many years after exposure / people might have asbestosis for a long time without dying ***[1 mark]***. (Therefore) the annual death rate from asbestosis might be rising while the people who had already been exposed to asbestos before the ban die ***[1 mark]***. Another explanation for the increase could be that doctors are getting better at diagnosing asbestosis or identifying it as a cause of death ***[1 mark]***.
***[Maximum of 4 marks available]***

## Pages 46-49: More Exchange and Transport Systems — 1

1.1 Any of the peptide bonds that are not at the end of the protein, e.g.

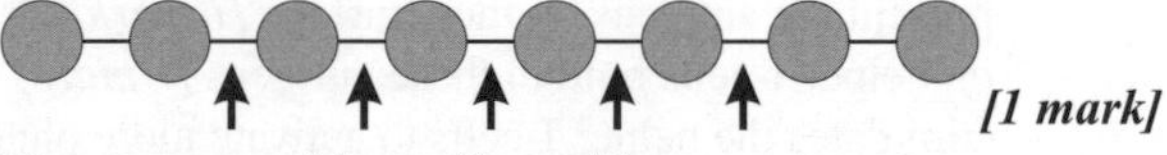

***[1 mark]***

1.2 Name: exopeptidases ***[1 mark]***
Function: they hydrolyse peptide bonds at the ends of proteins ***[1 mark]***.
Name: dipeptidases ***[1 mark]***
Function: they hydrolyse peptide bonds in dipeptides ***[1 mark]***.

1.3 E.g. amino acids are absorbed into the ileum epithelial cells by co-transport ***[1 mark]***. This involves sodium ions being actively transported from the ileum epithelial cells into the bloodstream ***[1 mark]***. This builds up a concentration gradient of sodium ions, with a higher concentration of sodium ions in the lumen of the ileum than in the ileum epithelial cells ***[1 mark]***. Sodium ions then diffuse into the ileum epithelial cells through sodium-dependent transporter proteins ***[1 mark]*** carrying amino acids with them ***[1 mark]***.

1.4 Without enteropeptidase, trypsin is not produced ***[1 mark]***, which means that proteins cannot be fully digested ***[1 mark]***. This may mean that not enough amino acids can be absorbed into the blood and used by body cells to keep the person healthy ***[1 mark]***.

2.1 Lipase A is an enzyme with an active site that has a specific shape ***[1 mark]*** that is more complementary to the shape of Type B oil molecules than Type A or Type C oil molecules ***[1 mark]***.

2.2 17.3 (Type B) ÷ 7.4 (Type C) = 2.3378...
**2.3** : 1 ***[1 mark]***

*When a calculation gives you a number with a lot of decimal places, give your answer to the lowest number of significant figures that was used in the measurements for the calculation.*

2.3 bile salts ***[1 mark]***

2.4 monoglycerides ***[1 mark]***
fatty acids ***[1 mark]***

2.5 Micelles move the monoglycerides and fatty acids/products of lipid digestion towards the epithelial lining of the small intestine ***[1 mark]***. As micelles break up, they release the monoglycerides and fatty acids/products of lipid digestion ***[1 mark]***. Both monoglycerides and fatty acids/the products of lipid digestion are then able to freely diffuse across the epithelial cell membrane ***[1 mark]***.

3.1 E.g. by setting up the equipment in the same way, but using the same volume of distilled water in the Visking tubing instead of amylase ***[1 mark]***.

3.2 Any two from: e.g. In a real gut there are transporters/protein channels for active transport of food molecules across the gut wall ***[1 mark]***. / Visking tubing doesn't have as large a surface area as the real gut ***[1 mark]***. / The real gut is surrounded by blood that maintains a concentration gradient ***[1 mark]***.

3.3 At the start of the experiment, the iodine test was positive for the Visking tubing contents, showing starch was present ***[1 mark]*** because it hadn't been digested by amylase yet ***[1 mark]***. The iodine test was negative for the beaker contents because the starch molecules were too big to fit through the Visking tubing membrane and move into the beaker ***[1 mark]***. At the end of the experiment, the iodine test was negative for the Visking tubing and the beaker contents because all the starch had been digested ***[1 mark]***.

3.4 At the start of the experiment, the Benedict's test was negative for both the Visking tubing and beaker contents showing there was no sugar present ***[1 mark]*** because the starch hadn't been digested into maltose yet ***[1 mark]***. At the end of the experiment, the Benedict's test was positive for the Visking tubing contents because the starch had been broken down into maltose ***[1 mark]***. The Benedict's test was also positive for the beaker contents because the maltose molecules were small enough to move through the Visking tubing membrane and into the beaker ***[1 mark]***.

## Pages 50-52: More Exchange and Transport Systems — 2

1.1 Any five from: at low partial pressures of oxygen, the percentage saturation of haemoglobin with oxygen is low ***[1 mark]*** because the four polypeptide chains that make up haemoglobin are tightly bound, making it difficult for oxygen to bind ***[1 mark]***. The curve rises steeply at medium partial pressures, as more haemoglobin is carrying oxygen ***[1 mark]***. This is because once the first oxygen has bound, haemoglobin changes shape, making it easier for additional oxygen molecules to bind ***[1 mark]***. At high partial pressures, the curve levels off/plateaus because more haemoglobin is saturated with oxygen ***[1 mark]***, so it gets harder for oxygen molecules to bind ***[1 mark]***. ***[Maximum of 5 marks available]***

1.2 Llamas live at high altitudes where there is less oxygen ***[1 mark]***, which means their haemoglobin has to have a higher affinity for oxygen than humans ***[1 mark]***. This puts the llama oxygen dissociation curve to the left of the human curve, because their haemoglobin loads more oxygen at lower partial pressures ***[1 mark]***.

1.3 The respiration rate increases during exercise, which increases the partial pressure of carbon dioxide in the blood ***[1 mark]***. Higher concentrations of carbon dioxide increase the rate of oxygen unloading and the saturation of blood with oxygen is lower for a given $pO_2$ ***[1 mark]***. This is called the Bohr effect ***[1 mark]***.

2.1 Name of X = aorta ***[1 mark]***
Name of Y = pulmonary vein ***[1 mark]***

2.2 Any three from: e.g. wear gloves ***[1 mark]*** / wear a lab coat ***[1 mark]*** / disinfect the area and equipment afterwards ***[1 mark]*** / take care with the use of sharp equipment ***[1 mark]***.

2.3 Any one from: e.g. use clear, continuous lines/no overlaps in lines ***[1 mark]*** / no shading ***[1 mark]*** / draw different components in proportion ***[1 mark]*** / include a scale ***[1 mark]*** / include relevant labels ***[1 mark]***.

3.1 Inflammation and thrombosis in small and medium arteries would lead to reduced blood flow to the fingers and toes ***[1 mark]***. Without an adequate supply of oxygen/glucose/nutrients etc., the tissue in the fingers and toes may die ***[1 mark]***.

3.2 At the start of a capillary bed, the hydrostatic pressure inside the capillaries is higher than outside ***[1 mark]***, so fluid is forced out of the capillaries, forming tissue fluid ***[1 mark]***. At the venule end of the capillary bed, the loss of fluid means the water potential inside the capillaries is lower than in the tissue fluid ***[1 mark]***, so some of the water in the tissue fluid re-enters the capillaries ***[1 mark]*** by osmosis ***[1 mark]***.

3.3 E.g. capillaries have walls that are only one cell thick, which shortens the diffusion pathway ***[1 mark]***.

## Pages 53-55: More Exchange and Transport Systems — 3

1.1 They prevent the backflow of blood *[1 mark]* into the atria when the ventricles contract *[1 mark]*.

1.2 They open when pressure is greater below the valve / in the ventricle than in the artery *[1 mark]*.

1.3

| | Standing up | Lying down |
|---|---|---|
| Mean heart rate / bpm | 74 | 57 |
| Mean cardiac output / $cm^3$ $min^{-1}$ | 4700 | 4700 |
| Mean stroke volume / $cm^3$ | 63.5 (3 s.f.) | 82.5 (3 s.f.) |

*[1 mark]*

*Stroke volume = cardiac output ÷ heart rate, so when standing up it's 4700 ÷ 74 = 63.5, and when lying down it's 4700 ÷ 57 = 82.5.*

1.4 It gives the heart rate time to stabilise, as the act of changing position could cause it to increase *[1 mark]*.

1.5 Heart rate is lower when lying down as blood does not have to be pumped above the level of the heart / against gravity *[1 mark]*.

*The heart has to work harder when a person is standing up, because blood has to flow against gravity. When you're lying down, the force of gravity is evenly distributed across the body.*

1.6 Taking multiple measurements and calculating the mean reduces the effect of random error, so makes the results more precise *[1 mark]*.

2.1 60 ÷ 0.55 = 109.0909...
**109** beats per minute *[1 mark]*

2.2 0.13 seconds or 0.68 seconds *[1 mark]*

*The left atrium contracts before the left ventricle in the cardiac cycle, so you need to find a point on the graph where the pressure of the atrium increases before the pressure of the ventricle increases.*

2.3 Any six from: at point A, pressure in the left ventricle exceeds pressure in the left atrium *[1 mark]*, because the left ventricle is contracting and the left atrium is relaxing *[1 mark]*. This causes the atrioventricular valve/the valve between the left atrium and left ventricle to close, preventing the backflow of blood into the left atrium *[1 mark]*.
At point B, pressure increases in the left ventricle to above that of the aorta *[1 mark]*, which forces the semi-lunar valve/the valve between the left ventricle and aorta open *[1 mark]*.
At point C, the left ventricular pressure falls below that of the aorta *[1 mark]*, because blood has moved into the aorta from the ventricle and the left ventricle is relaxing *[1 mark]*. As a result, the semi-lunar valve/the valve between the left ventricle and the aorta closes *[1 mark]*.
Finally, at point D, pressure has been increasing in the left atrium as blood has been returning to the atrium from the body *[1 mark]*. As the atrial pressure exceeds ventricular pressure *[1 mark]*, the atrioventricular valve/valve between the left atrium and left ventricle opens, allowing blood to flow into the left ventricle *[1 mark]*.
***[Maximum of 6 marks available]***

2.4 The left ventricle has a higher maximum pressure than the left atrium because it has a thicker muscle wall and so is able to generate more force when it contracts *[1 mark]*.

2.5 The wall of the aorta is thick and muscular / the wall of the aorta contains elastic tissue to stretch and recoil / the inner lining of the aorta is folded so it can stretch *[1 mark]*, which helps to maintain the high pressure of the blood coming out of the left ventricle *[1 mark]*.

## Pages 56-58: More Exchange and Transport Systems — 4

1.1 Water on the leaves would reduce the water potential gradient between inside the leaf and outside *[1 mark]*, reducing water loss/transpiration *[1 mark]*.

1.2 The higher the temperature, the faster the rate of transpiration *[1 mark]*. At higher temperatures, water molecules have more kinetic energy so they evaporate more quickly from the cells inside the leaf *[1 mark]*. This increases the water potential/concentration gradient between the inside and outside of the leaf, so water diffuses out of the leaf faster *[1 mark]*.

2.1 Light intensity is higher at 12:00, so more stomata are open *[1 mark]*, which increases the transpiration rate *[1 mark]*. This draws water molecules up the xylem at a quicker rate, due to cohesion and tension *[1 mark]*.

*At 00:00, it would be dark, whereas there is sunlight at 12:00.*

2.2 To prevent the plant tissue from drying out *[1 mark]*.

2.3 Dyeing the tissue with a stain/named stain *[1 mark]*.

3.1 Translocation requires energy/ATP *[1 mark]*. If metabolism stops, respiration cannot occur so ATP is not produced / energy is not released *[1 mark]*.

3.2 The level of pressure at point A is higher than that at point B *[1 mark]*. This is because, at point A, the water potential is being lowered by the solutes entering from the companion cell, causing water to enter from the xylem and companion cell *[1 mark]*, and raising the pressure *[1 mark]*.

3.3 The concentration of solutes at point A would increase because the solutes are still being loaded from the companion cell and can't flow down the phloem *[1 mark]*, as phloem is removed when a ring of bark is taken *[1 mark]*.

3.4 E.g. in a tracer experiment, a leaf could be supplied with radioactively labelled $CO_2$ *[1 mark]*, which would then be incorporated into the organic substances produced by the leaf *[1 mark]*. The movement of these substances around the plant could then be tracked by detecting the radioactively labelled carbon *[1 mark]*.

# Topic Four — Genetic Information and Variation

## Pages 59-62: DNA, RNA and Protein Synthesis

1.1 The DNA is wound around histone proteins *[1 mark]* and then tightly coiled into compact chromosomes *[1 mark]*.

1.2 Any one from: e.g. prokaryotic DNA is not associated with proteins *[1 mark]*. / Prokaryotic DNA is condensed by supercoiling *[1 mark]*.

1.3 The total length of DNA is 2 m.
1.5% of the DNA encodes proteins.
Therefore, (1.5 ÷ 100) × 2 = 0.03 m of DNA corresponds to protein-encoding genes.
There are 20 000 protein-encoding genes.
Therefore, the average length of a gene is:
0.03 ÷ 20 000 = **0.0000015 m** or **$1.5 \times 10^{-6}$ m**
***[2 marks for the correct answer, 1 mark for 0.03 m]***

1.4 genome *[1 mark]*

1.5 proteome *[1 mark]*

1.6 E.g. prokaryotes don't have introns/non-coding sequences within genes ***[1 mark]***. Prokaryotes have shorter/fewer multiple repeat sequences between genes ***[1 mark]***.

1.7 E.g. genes encoding ribosomal RNA ***[1 mark]***. Genes encoding tRNAs ***[1 mark]***.

2.1 Any two from: e.g. mitochondrial DNA is shorter while the DNA in the nucleus is longer ***[1 mark]***. / Mitochondrial DNA is circular while the DNA in the nucleus is linear ***[1 mark]***. / Mitochondrial DNA is not associated with proteins, while DNA in the nucleus is associated with proteins/histones ***[1 mark]***.

2.2 D ***[1 mark]***

2.3 E.g. valine is coded for by four DNA codons ***[1 mark]***.

*'Degenerate' means that multiple DNA codons can code for one amino acid, so any evidence that shows this from the table could gain a mark.*

2.4 The mRNA codon GAC will become GCC / an A at mRNA codon position 156 will be swapped for a C ***[1 mark]***.

2.5 An arginine amino acid will be produced at position 156 instead of a leucine ***[1 mark]***.

2.6 It could change the shape of the enzyme ***[1 mark]*** so that the substrate is no longer able to fit into its active site ***[1 mark]***, preventing the enzyme from being able to catalyse the reaction ***[1 mark]***.

2.7 Any five from: e.g. the mRNA attaches to a ribosome ***[1 mark]***. tRNA molecules carry amino acids to the ribosome ***[1 mark]***. The tRNAs attach to the mRNA via complementary/specific base pairing ***[1 mark]***. The amino acids on adjacent tRNAs join together with peptide bonds ***[1 mark]***. ATP provides the energy for peptide bond formation ***[1 mark]***. The ribosome moves along the mRNA and the amino acid chain is extended ***[1 mark]***. The process continues until a stop signal on the mRNA is reached ***[1 mark]***. ***[Maximum of 5 marks available]***

3.1 Any four from: e.g. after the DNA has been unwound ***[1 mark]***, RNA polymerase lines up free RNA nucleotides along the template strand ***[1 mark]*** according to the rules of complementary base pairing ***[1 mark]***. RNA polymerase then joins the RNA nucleotides together as it moves along the DNA template strand ***[1 mark]***. Once RNA polymerase reaches a stop signal, it detaches and the mRNA is released ***[1 mark]***. ***[Maximum of 4 marks available]***

3.2 The original DNA contains introns, while the cDNA does not / the cDNA only contains exons ***[1 mark]***. This is because the cDNA is made from mRNA, which has been spliced / had the introns removed ***[1 mark]***.

3.3 The levels of mRNAs 2 and 3 were only slightly affected by the drug ***[1 mark]***. If RNA polymerase was inhibited, the levels of all of the mRNAs would have decreased by a large amount ***[1 mark]***.

3.4 Only the level of mRNA 1 has been significantly reduced ***[1 mark]***. This indicates that mRNA 1 contains the particular sequence destroyed by the drug ***[1 mark]***.

## Pages 63-65: Diversity, Classification and Variation — 1

1.1 A species is a group of similar organisms able to reproduce to give fertile offspring ***[1 mark]***.

1.2 four ***[1 mark]***

*The genera shown on the phylogenetic tree are* Panthera, Meles, Lutra *and* Canis. *You know that these are the genera because the binomial name for a species is made up of two parts, e.g.* Panthera leo, *and the first part is always the genus.*

1.3 *Canis aureus* and *Canis lupus* because they both belong to the same genus ***[1 mark]***.

1.4 Family ***[1 mark]***

2.1 Both types of selection increase the likelihood of organisms with the beneficial traits surviving ***[1 mark]***. However, the selection acting on population A increases the chances of organisms with an extreme phenotype surviving ***[1 mark]***, whereas the selection acting on population B increases the chance of organisms with an average trait surviving ***[1 mark]***.

2.2 Population A, because this is showing directional selection / selection for an extreme phenotype ***[1 mark]***. Taller plants are likely to be selected for in dense forest because these could more easily gain access to sunlight ***[1 mark]***.

2.3 E.g. the environmental conditions in the grassland and the forest are different. / In an open field, being too tall would be a disadvantage due to the risk of damage by wind. ***[1 mark]***

2.4 E.g. if a female lays too many eggs then she may be unable to care for them all ***[1 mark]***. If she doesn't lay enough eggs then there is a chance that no chicks would survive to adulthood ***[1 mark]***. So, an intermediate number of eggs is selected for, and variation in the clutch size decreases over time ***[1 mark]***.

*Figure 3 shows that clutch size is undergoing stabilising selection — the mean stays roughly the same, but variation (shown by the error bars) is decreasing.*

3.1 Proteins consists of amino acids which are encoded by DNA base sequences ***[1 mark]***. The more similar the proteins are, the more similar the DNA is between two species ***[1 mark]***, and so the more closely related they are ***[1 mark]***.

3.2 Species A is the least closely related to humans, as it has the greatest number of differences in amino acid sequence from the human protein ***[1 mark]***. Species C is the most closely related to humans as it's amino acid sequence has the fewest differences ***[1 mark]***.

3.3 E.g. both species have seven differences in their amino acid sequence from the human protein, but they could be unique differences / at different points in the sequence, so you can't tell how closely related they are to each other ***[1 mark]***.

## Pages 66-69: Diversity, Classification and Variation — 2

1.1

| Species | Number of individual plants counted in different quadrats | | | | | Mean number counted |
|---|---|---|---|---|---|---|
| Rapeseed | 24 | 46 | 32 | 28 | 32 | **32.4** |
| Common sunflower | 1 | 0 | 2 | 1 | 1 | **1** |
| Common poppy | 8 | 12 | 6 | 10 | 8 | **8.8** |
| Creeping thistle | 13 | 14 | 7 | 15 | 13 | **12.4** |

***[1 mark]***

1.2 $N = 32.4 + 1 + 8.8 + 12.4$
$= 54.6$

$$d = \frac{54.6(54.6-1)}{32.4(32.4-1)+1(1-1)+8.8(8.8-1)+12.4(12.4-1)}$$

$$= \frac{2926.6}{1227.4}$$

$d =$ **2.38** (to 3 s.f.)

***[2 marks for the correct answer, otherwise 1 mark for $N(N-1) = 2926.6$ or $\Sigma n(n-1) = 1227.4$. Allow full marks if incorrect answers to 1.1 used correctly.]***

1.3 The scientists could have used a t-test ***[1 mark]*** as this would have allowed them to compare two mean values ***[1 mark]***.

1.4 E.g. animal grazing prevents some plants from growing, reducing plant biodiversity ***[1 mark]***. This would mean there are fewer habitats and food resources to support other organisms, further reducing biodiversity ***[1 mark]***.

2.1 Because an index of diversity takes into account both the number of species and the number of individuals ***[1 mark]***, which means that it takes into account species that are only present in small numbers, which species richness does not ***[1 mark]***.

2.2 Any three from: e.g. there were fewer ladybird species on the conventional farm than on the organic farm. / The standard deviation bars do not overlap, so the difference was significant/the standard deviation bars are short, showing that the data is precise. / However, there is no indication of how many samples were taken, so the data may not be representative of all organic/conventional farms. / There may be factors other than the way in which the fields were farmed, which influenced the number of ladybird species present. / The scientists' conclusion is correct for this data, but further investigation is needed to ensure that these results are valid ***[1 mark for each correct answer]***.

2.3 E.g. the scientists could have taken random samples, to prevent sampling bias ***[1 mark]***. / They could have had a large sample size, to reduce the risk of results being due to chance ***[1 mark]***.

3.1 To sterilise it ***[1 mark]*** and prevent contamination of the investigation which could affect the results ***[1 mark]***.

3.2 Any five from: e.g. disinfect work surfaces/wash hands to prevent contamination of cultures ***[1 mark]***. Work near a Bunsen burner flame ***[1 mark]***. Flame the neck of the glass bottle of bacterial culture just before use ***[1 mark]***. Use a sterile pipette to transfer the bacteria from the broth to the agar plate ***[1 mark]***. Spread the bacteria over the plate using a sterile plastic spreader ***[1 mark]***. Soak a paper disc in each type of hand sanitiser and use sterile forceps to place each disc on the plate ***[1 mark]***. Lightly tape a lid onto the plate ***[1 mark]***. Invert and incubate at 25 °C for 48 hours ***[1 mark]***. ***[Maximum of 5 marks available]***

3.3 To act as a control ***[1 mark]*** and ensure that it was only the antibacterial hand sanitiser that was preventing growth, and not the paper disc itself ***[1 mark]***.

3.4

| Disc | Area of Inhibition Zone / $mm^2$ |
|---|---|
| B | **346** (to 3 s.f.) |
| C | **908** (to 3 s.f.) |
| D | **227** (to 3 s.f.) |

***[1 mark]***

4.1 The crossing over of homologous chromosomes in meiosis I ***[1 mark]*** leads to the four daughter cells containing different combinations of alleles ***[1 mark]***. Independent segregation in meiosis I ***[1 mark]*** leads to the daughter cells containing any combination of maternal and paternal chromosomes ***[1 mark]***.

4.2 $n = 23$ in humans
$2^{23} =$ **8 388 608** ***[1 mark]***

4.3 Non-disjunction ***[1 mark]*** means that chromosome 13 ***[1 mark]*** fails to separate properly during meiosis, leaving one daughter cell/gamete with an extra copy of chromosome 13 and another with no copies ***[1 mark]***. If a gamete with an extra copy of chromosome 13 is fertilised, the resulting zygote will have three copies, leading to Patau syndrome ***[1 mark]***.

## Pages 70-72: Diversity, Classification and Variation — 3

1.1 For species A, B, D and E, there is a less than 5% probability that the results are due to chance ***[1 mark]***. For species C, there is a greater than 5% probability that the results are due to chance ***[1 mark]***.

1.2 Any two from: e.g. the time of year the traps were set. / The length of time the traps were left for. / The depth at which the traps were set. / The type of traps used. / The age/size of the fish caught. / The health of the fish caught. ***[2 marks — 1 mark for each correct answer]***

1.3 E.g. the scientists could have compared the DNA/mRNA base sequence of the same gene in different individual fish ***[1 mark]***. This would have allowed them to estimate the number of different alleles the population has for that particular gene, giving them an indication of genetic diversity ***[1 mark]***.

1.4 E.g. it allows natural selection to take place. / It allows the population to adapt to environmental changes. ***[1 mark]***

2.1 E.g. from 0 to approximately 15 $\mu g\ cm^{-3}$, the number of strain B bacteria decreases more rapidly with increasing ampicillin concentration than the number of strain A bacteria ***[1 mark]***. Above an ampicillin concentration of approximately 15 $\mu g\ cm^{-3}$, the number of strain A bacteria remains fairly constant at about 1000 cells, but the number of strain B continues to decrease. ***[1 mark]***

2.2 E.g. ionising radiation is a mutagenic agent / increases the chance of mutations arising ***[1 mark]***. A mutation may have caused the active site of the strain A transpeptidase to change shape ***[1 mark]***, so that ampicillin could no longer bind to and inhibit the enzyme ***[1 mark]***. So strain A bacteria with the mutation were more likely to survive and reproduce in increasing ampicillin concentrations than strain B bacteria ***[1 mark]***.

3.1 Courtship behaviours are species-specific ***[1 mark]***. They allow organisms to recognise members of their own species ***[1 mark]***, to ensure that mating leads to the production of fertile offspring ***[1 mark]***.

3.2 As a result of mutation, some males had an allele/alleles for larger horn size ***[1 mark]***. These males would have had a greater chance of defeating their rivals during fights over females ***[1 mark]***, so they would have been more likely to reproduce and pass on their beneficial alleles to the next generation ***[1 mark]***. After many generations, the frequency of the allele/alleles for large horn size would have increased in the population of male wild bighorn sheep ***[1 mark]***.

3.3 Stabilising selection ***[1 mark]***. The hunting exerts a selection pressure against large horns ***[1 mark]*** but there is still selection pressure against small horns, due to males fighting for mates ***[1 mark]***.

3.4 E.g. the wild sheep have a greater genetic diversity than the agricultural sheep ***[1 mark]***. This means that the wild population can more easily withstand environmental changes / a new disease arriving ***[1 mark]***.

### Pages 73-74: Diversity, Classification and Variation — 4

1.1 E.g. if three consecutive bases were deleted/a base triplet was deleted, the amino acid they/it coded for would be lost ***[1 mark]***.

1.2 A change in the amino acid sequence could affect the tertiary structure of the CFTR protein ***[1 mark]***. This could impair the function of the protein, and affect the transport of chloride ions across cell membranes in the lungs ***[1 mark]***. This could affect the water potential of the cells in the lungs, leading to increased water absorption ***[1 mark]***.

1.3 E.g. the effect of the mutations on the amino acid sequence of the CFTR protein and its tertiary structure is relatively minor ***[1 mark]*** and therefore the function of the CFTR protein is less impaired ***[1 mark]***.

2.1 $0.7 \times 0.5 \times 0.4 \times 0.6 =$ **0.084** ***[1 mark]***

2.2 To prevent members of different species from mating ***[1 mark]***, as only females of the correct species will respond to a particular birdsong ***[1 mark]***.

2.3 Both the populations have a similar pattern of courtship behaviour / the same courtship behaviours in roughly the same sequence ***[1 mark]***, which suggests that they are closely related ***[1 mark]***. However, there are key differences in their behaviour, e.g. preening females is an important step for the first population, but doesn't directly lead to mating in the second population / bobbing the head can lead to mating in the second population but not in the first ***[1 mark]***. These differences suggest that the two are separate species / may be becoming two separate species ***[1 mark]***.

2.4 It may mean that only a limited number of males get to mate and pass on their alleles ***[1 mark]***, so the number of alleles in the gene pool decreases ***[1 mark]***.

## Mixed Questions

### Pages 75-80: Mixed Questions

1.1 D ***[1 mark]***

1.2 E.g. the reaction/breakdown of lactose is a hydrolysis reaction ***[1 mark]***, which requires the addition of a water molecule ***[1 mark]***.

1.3 E.g. that lactase is only active below pH 8 / lactase is inactive at pH 8 or above ***[1 mark]***. Lactase breaks lactose down into glucose and galactose ***[1 mark]***. Therefore, if glucose is present/the strip is green, it indicates lactase is active / if glucose is absent/the strip is yellow, it indicates that lactase is inactive ***[1 mark]***.

1.4 Above and below its optimum pH, every enzyme is affected by the $H^+$ and $OH^-$ ions found in acids and alkalis ***[1 mark]***. These ions interfere with the ionic and hydrogen bonds that hold the enzyme's tertiary structure together ***[1 mark]***. This changes the shape of the enzyme's active site ***[1 mark]***.

1.5 Any two from: e.g. the temperature of the solutions. / The concentration of the lactose and lactase solutions. / The type of glucose test strip used. / The person observing the colour change of each glucose test strip. ***[2 marks available — 1 mark for each reasonable suggestion]***

*For this question there are other correct answers that aren't listed here. For an answer to be valid, the variable needs to have an impact on the results, and be something that's possible to control in an experiment.*

1.6 E.g. increase the number of reactions carried out between pH 7 and 8 ***[1 mark]*** because it is between these pH values that lactase activity stops ***[1 mark]***.

*Accurate results need to be close to the true answer, so increasing the number of reactions carried out between pH 7 and 8 would let the student narrow down where lactase activity stops. E.g. the investigation could show that the activity stops between pH 7.2 and 7.3 rather than between pH 7 and 8.*

1.7 E.g. it allows the breakdown products of lactose to be immediately absorbed from the ileum into bloodstream ***[1 mark]***.

1.8 E.g. the mutation produced an allele which increased people's chance of survival in Europe ***[1 mark]***. This meant individuals with the mutation were more likely to survive, reproduce and pass on the beneficial allele to the next generation ***[1 mark]***. The frequency of this allele increased from generation to generation in the European population ***[1 mark]***.

2.1 spindle fibre ***[1 mark]***

2.2 Cell B because the diagram shows the homologous pairs being separated, not the sister chromatids ***[1 mark]***.

2.3 20 ***[1 mark]***

2.4 Meiosis because the chromosome number changes from diploid/2n in the sporophyte to haploid/n in the spores ***[1 mark]***.

2.5 When a sperm fertilises an egg, a diploid/2n fertilised gametophyte is formed ***[1 mark]***. This must mean that both the egg and sperm are haploid/n ***[1 mark]***. The spores are also haploid/n and to maintain a haploid number of chromosomes between the spores and gametophytes, stages 1 and 2 must represent mitosis ***[1 mark]***.

3.1 $Cl^-$ ions move from the epithelial cells lining the ileum, through the open $Cl^-$ channel proteins and into the ileum lumen ***[1 mark]***. The build up of $Cl^-$ ions lowers the water potential of the lumen ***[1 mark]***. This causes water to move by osmosis out of the epithelial cells into the lumen ***[1 mark]***. This lowers the water potential of the epithelial cells, causing water to move out of the blood into the cells ***[1 mark]***.

3.2 E.g. *V. cholerae* will have a cell wall, the ileum epithelial cell will not ***[1 mark]***. / *V. cholerae* will not have a nucleus/membrane-bound organelles, the ileum epithelial cell will ***[1 mark]***. / *V. cholerae* will have smaller ribosomes than the ileum epithelial cell ***[1 mark]***.

*You're being asked to compare the structure of a prokaryotic cell (V. cholerae) to that of a eukaryotic animal cell (the ileum epithelial cell) here.*

3.3 E.g. an attachment protein on HIV attaching to a receptor protein on a helper T-cell. ***[1 mark]***

3.4 Antigenic variation means that different strains of *V. cholerae* have different antigens ***[1 mark]***. Memory cells produced as a result of a past cholera infection won't recognise antigens of a different *V. cholerae* strain ***[1 mark]***. Therefore, there won't be a fast secondary response to the new strain/the person won't be immune to the new strain and they will become ill with cholera again ***[1 mark]***.

4.1 E.g. homogenisation could be used to break open the cells and release their contents into solution ***[1 mark]***. Ultracentrifugation could then be carried out to separate the proteins in the cells from the solution ***[1 mark]***.

4.2 To prevent antibodies binding non-specifically to the protein-binding sites on the membrane ***[1 mark]***.

4.3 In infected individuals, the HBV proteins/antigens will have been detected by the immune system ***[1 mark]***. This will have led to the activation of B-cells with an antibody complementary to the HBV antigen ***[1 mark]***. Each activated B-cell will have divided into plasma cells, which produced antibodies against the HBV proteins/antigens ***[1 mark]***.

4.4 At a higher temperature the enzyme may denature and fail to catalyse the reaction / produce a colour change ***[1 mark]***.

4.5 If the individual is not infected with HBV, their blood will not contain any antibodies that bind to HBV proteins ***[1 mark]***. As a result, after the first washing step, there will be no antibodies bound to the membrane for the secondary antibodies to bind to ***[1 mark]***. This means that there will be no HRP present after the second washing step to catalyse the colour changing reaction and no bands will be observed ***[1 mark]***.

BAQ51